The Young Adult's Guide to

STOP
BULLYING

Understanding Bullies and Their Actions

Rebekah Sack

The Young Adult's Guide to Stop Bullying: Understanding Bullies and Their Actions

Copyright © 2016 by Atlantic Publishing Group, Inc.
1405 SW 6th Ave. • Ocala, Florida 34471 • 800-814-1132 • 352-622-1875–Fax
Web site: www.atlantic-pub.com • E-mail: sales@atlantic-pub.com
SAN Number: 268-1250

Library of Congress Cataloging-in-Publication Data

Names: Atlantic Publishing Group.
Title: The young adult's guide to stop bullying : understanding bullies and
   their actions / by Rebekah Sack
Other titles: Guide to stop bullying
Description: Ocala, Florida : Atlantic Publishing Group, Inc., 2016. |
   Audience: Grade 9 to 12. | Includes bibliographical references and index.
Identifiers: LCCN 2015037911| ISBN 9781601389886 (alk. paper) | ISBN
   1601389884 (alk. paper)
Subjects: LCSH: Bullying--Juvenile literature. |
   Bullying--Prevention--Juvenile literature.
Classification: LCC BF637.B85 .Y678 2015 | DDC 302.34/3--dc23 LC record available at
http://lccn.loc.gov/2015037911

Printed on Recycled Paper

Printed in the United States

Reduce. Reuse.
RECYCLE.

A decade ago, Atlantic Publishing signed the Green Press Initiative. These guidelines promote environmentally friendly practices, such as using recycled stock and vegetable-based inks, avoiding waste, choosing energy-efficient resources, and promoting a no-pulping policy. We now use 100-percent recycled stock on all our books. The results: in one year, switching to post-consumer recycled stock saved 24 mature trees, 5,000 gallons of water, the equivalent of the total energy used for one home in a year, and the equivalent of the greenhouse gases from one car driven for a year.

Over the years, we have adopted a number of dogs from rescues and shelters. First there was Bear and after he passed, Ginger and Scout. Now, we have Kira, another rescue. They have brought immense joy and love into not just into our lives, but into the lives of all who met them.

We want you to know a portion of the profits of this book will be donated in Bear, Ginger and Scout's memory to local animal shelters, parks, conservation organizations, and other individuals and nonprofit organizations in need of assistance.

– Douglas & Sherri Brown,
President & Vice-President of Atlantic Publishing

Table of Contents

Part II: You See Bullying 95

Part III: You're a Bully **127**

Introduction

Take one.

You're in the locker room, in your usual corner. You're getting ready to change, but you hesitate, as always, taking a moment to look around you to see if anyone is staring at you.

Your insecurity is heavy today, the weight of your bones fuller than normal. You turn back around and begin to lift your shirt.

You hear a snicker behind you, but you don't turn around. You want to keep your body facing the wall, because you've always hated the way your stomach looks.

You hear the click of a phone unlocking.

Heart pounding, knees locking, chest rising and falling faster than ever.

A flash reflects off the glistening red locker, and you hear muffled sounds, hands on mouths covering the melody of mocking laughs from the popular kids.

They've taken a picture of you. You quickly put your gym shirt on and rush to the bathroom stall to give your stinging eyes some relief.

What Is Bullying?

If you go to school, you've probably seen some type of bullying. Maybe it was the crunch of a knuckle on a nose. Maybe it was the overweight outcast being taunted by her locker — "how's it goin' big mama?" Maybe it was the popular girl pretending to be interested in the nerdy kid, just so she could make fun of the fact that he thought she was serious (Me? Interested in you? Ha!).

Even if you don't go to school, you've probably seen some type of cyber-bullying. Bullying on the Internet isn't just something that happens to people your age — adults are doing it, too.

If you've been bullied, you know the effect it can have on your day-to-day life. You're used to the upset stomach in the morning because the thought of going to school is actually making you sick (I swear I'm not faking it, mom!).

Let me tell you now — you aren't alone. Here are some quick facts about bullying:

- According to the award-winning weekly PBS teen series, "In the Mix," up to 25 percent of United States students are bullied each year.
- As many as 160,000 children stay at home from school on any given day out of the fear of being bullied.

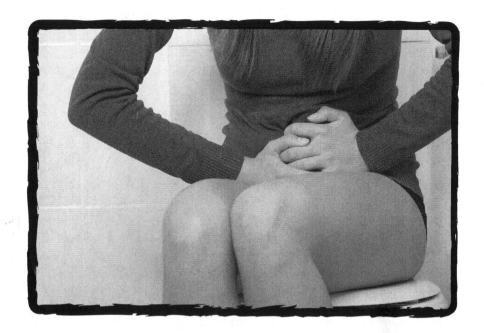

- At least one out of three teenagers say they have been seriously threatened online.

Teasing

Many people are confused by the term "bullying." Some don't see things like teasing and mocking as bullying; they see physical harm as bullying. Others don't realize that a lot of bullying going on is happening on the Internet, which is now called "cyberbullying."

Bullying isn't something that happens just once. It's something that happens all the time. Bullying is hurting someone on purpose — the bully enjoys inflicting harm.

When we say, "hurting someone," we don't just mean physical abuse (as in a punch or a kick). This includes verbal abuse, which means hurting someone with your words (as in telling someone they're ugly or making fun of their clothing).

If you're still not really understanding what bullying is, here is a list that gives some common examples. You might see something on the list and think, "Hey, that's happened to me," or even, "oh my gosh, I've done that."

- Verbal abuse and harassment
- Telling someone they can't be a part of a group (on purpose)
- Spreading rumors that aren't true
- Sending another person mean or threatening notes
- Making harassing, threatening phone calls

- Sending mean or threatening emails
- Actively encouraging a peer group to dislike and isolate another person
- Physical abuse
- Making continual threats to harm another person and/or their family
- Stealing or destroying another person's property
- Playing "pranks" on another person in front of his or her peer group
- "Visual" abuse, e.g., making obscene gestures to another person
- Drawing obscene or humiliating graffiti about another person
- Continually using humiliating racial slurs towards another person
- Touching another person and/or making sexual comments
- Mobbing, i.e., several bullies act in concert to harm another person
- Completely and pointedly annoying another person
- Frightening another person through physical or emotional intimidation
- Forcing another person to do something he or she does not want to do
- Stalking the victim, instilling fear, rage, and helplessness into the victim's everyday life

Some of these examples are extreme (stalking someone or physically hurting them). If you look close enough, you'll see some examples that seem relatively harmless (playing pranks or spreading rumors).

Think about your years in school. Have you ever heard something shocking (Did you hear that Abby lost her virginity?) and then told one of your friends about it? Odds are you probably have — none of us are perfect.

The point is, bullying is bigger than a lot of us think, and it affects people in profound ways (bullying makes you sweat more? what?).

What Is Cyberbullying?

The birth of technology has done amazing things for the world — it has made communicating a whole lot easier among other things.

But if you think about it, the bullies of 50 years ago didn't have it, which can explain why bullying has become such a big problem.

Technology has a dark side. Because of this, bullies can now hurt people from the comfort of their bed, and without having to deal with anyone face-to-face (ever seen the movie "Easy A?").

Maybe you've experienced cyberbullying — it's really impersonal and distanced. There are a lot of ways you can cyberbully if you think about the different kinds of technology we have — cell phones, social media, computers, iPads, tablets, and even watches.

Before all of this stuff was invented, you could at least feel safe at home, away from the bullying. It used to be your safe haven. Now, that isn't the case. Everywhere you go, someone has the ability to bully you.

Cyberbullying isn't only about someone threatening you or harassing you online, either. It also includes embarrassment and humiliation. If someone is spreading a false rumor about you on the Internet, you are a victim of cyberbullying.

"Easy A" was mentioned earlier as an example of a movie that discusses cyberbullying, but maybe you've heard of another box office hit — "Mean Girls." Starring Lindsey Lohan, this movie is about an outcast trying to fit in in school. There's a scene in the movie that shows what is called the "three way calling attack," according to Rosalind Wiseman (qtd. in McGrath, 2002). Maybe you've seen it?

It goes a little like this: Girl A gets Girl B on the phone, then conferences-in Girl C without the knowledge of Girl B. Girl A, the cyberbully, then entices Girl B, the victim, to say bad things about Girl C, who just listens quietly. Girl B then finds herself ignored and ostracized from the group and has no idea why.

Blogs and websites are also created just to bully someone. Have you ever seen Rachel Ray, the famous chef, on television? If you look her up online, chances are you'll see some websites dedicated to talking trash about her. Sites like with names like "Rachel Ray Sucks" and "Why I Hate Rachel Ray" are everywhere, and anyone can make them. See — adults are being bullied, too.

There have been many famous cases of cyberbullying in the news, and you may have seen the deadly outcome. One of the first cases of cyberbullying was in 2003 with the tragic suicide of 13-year-old Ryan Halligan.

He was a "lanky" boy, "fumbling his way through early adolescence" (**www.ryanpatrickhalligan.org**). (Sound familiar?) Ryan was bullied all through school, and he dealt with it up until a certain point. He was trying to make friends, and thought he had befriended a pretty, popular girl in school. They started messaging each other on an instant messenger, and Ryan started opening up to her. It turns out that she was copying and pasting their messages to all her girlfriends, and they were having a good laugh at Ryan's expense.

Ryan hanged himself on October 7, 2003.

Megan Meier, also 13, took her own life after being harassed on MySpace; Tyler Clementi for being gay, Amanda Todd, Jessica Logan, Hope Witsell... the list goes on.

If you are being bullied online, you are definitely not alone, but you will learn everything you need to know in this book to arm yourself and everyone around you to stop the bullying.

You're going to learn things you can do to defend yourself, how to step in and stop bullies from hurting other people, and how to make a serious change — because you can.

It only takes one person to make a difference.

You're Being Bullied

Halifax, Nova Scotia, April 8, 2002. Fourteen-year-old Emmet Fralick, an outgoing, popular student, shot and killed himself. His suicide note stated that he could no longer tolerate being bullied by his peers. Investigations revealed that, on a regular basis, Emmet had been bullied by extortion, threats, and beatings from other students.

Emmet is just one of many who was bullied to the point of no return. In this section, we're going to a take a look at why people are at risk for bullying, the effects that bullying can have on a person, and most importantly, how you can defend yourself against bullies.

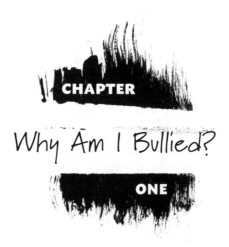

Why Am I Bullied?

So, you're being bullied.

People are bullied for many reasons, but all of these reasons have one thing in common: you're different in some way.

Being different is awesome — there are billions of people in the world. What if we were all the same? Have you ever read "Brave New World"? That image is pretty scary, right?

The other uncool thing about bullying is that there are so many reasons for why you could be bullied. It seems like you're more likely to be bullied than not these days.

Let's take a look at some common reasons on why you might be bullied. You may find that one of them describes you.

You're New

Being the new kid on the block is sure to turn some heads. When the principal announces that there's a new kid in school, everyone gets excited, especially in smaller schools. It's a change, and everyone's interested.

That means that all eyes are on you. Any wrong move can impact how people see you. Even if you don't make a wrong move, people may not like you, just because you're new (we know, it's cruel).

This concept of tormenting "the new kid" dates back to 1970.

CASE STUDY

Val, 54 years old

"When I was 8, my family moved to a then-rural part of Decatur, IL on a dead-end street. Finally, I thought, I'd be able to ride my bike without worrying about traffic.

And I did, for a short time, until a group of neighborhood teenagers decided it would be fun to make the new kid's life a living hell. The youngest was 13, the oldest 17, and there were five of them. Two were brother and sister and lived next door. Three were brothers who lived a couple of houses away. The oldest had a driver's license and access to a car.

They mostly rode their bikes or walked, and they blocked the street so I couldn't pass them. If I tried, they knocked me off my bike. They called me names. They threatened to hurt my dog and me. Sometimes, they rode in the car and he drove at me when I was on my bike, making me panic and go into the ditch. I was in actual fear for my safety, and if that 17-year-old boy, an inexperienced driver, had miscalculated even a little, he could have killed me.

My parents tried talking to their parents, whom you would think would be horrified that their teenagers were bullying a little girl, but they refused to listen or do anything to stop it. My parents tried calling the police, who for some reason also did nothing to stop it.

My only sibling is a much-older brother, who at that time was already an adult, and while he could cuss and threaten, he couldn't actually do anything to these teenagers, because he would have gotten arrested. If he'd only been a few years younger, he might have been able to do more to protect me. He did what he could. He got so angry with the one who could drive that he kicked a dent in the boy's car door.

But these kids, egged on by their parents, or at least not punished or restrained by them, continued to torment me.

As the new kid on the street, I didn't have any friends, and the kids I did play with were my age, which meant that they were wholly inadequate in size and strength to be of much help.

I was imprisoned in my own yard where the teenagers couldn't come, though with two of them living next door, they would even gather up in that family's yard and verbally torment me over the fence. My mother would stay outside with me as much as she could, and she and their mother got into more than one verbal confrontation over this behavior. Their mother witnessed the way they treated me and not only did nothing to stop them, but sometimes, she even joined in.

I was afraid to leave my yard, afraid even to go outdoors to play if those kids were anywhere around. I spent most of the first year we lived in that house as a timid, terrified captive to their cruelty.

Eventually, they tired of the sport of tormenting a little girl, and the bullying stopped. I made friends who went to school with them, and maybe that helped, too. I went to parochial school, and some of the verbal taunts were related to what a stuck-up snob I must be. To this day, I cannot imagine what possessed teenagers to torment a child that way, or why their parents allowed and even encouraged it."

You're Smart

What? People are making fun of me because I got an A on the Science test? They're calling me the "teacher's pet?"

It sounds crazy, we know, but it's happening everywhere. Here's how it works: you're really good at something. Other people see how good you are and realize that they aren't as good as you. They're jealous of you. They feel like they're inferior (not as good as you), so they start bullying you to bring you down.

It doesn't make much sense when you look at it for what it is, but when it's actually happening, it's very real. School should be about learning, but you know better than anyone that the social aspect of school is pretty important. How many friends you have, who you sit with at

lunch, how many people think you're cute — people talk about that stuff more than they talk about Chapter 6 of the history book.

You didn't have to study for finals week. You already know everything. School is really easy for you, and people are starting to notice.

You don't have to look far to see subtle hints of bullying when it comes to being bright. Many kids are made fun of just for reading — reading is perceived as nerdy, even though reading is said by many to be the key to success and intelligence.

It seems to be the same thing with Scholastic Bowl. You're fast and you're clever. Be proud of it. In ten years, when you're successful, you'll be glad you didn't dumb yourself down to fit in.

CASE STUDY

Students Speak Up

The Telegraph published an article in 2009 about young students dumbing themselves down so that they wouldn't be bullied. Many adults are probably thinking, "What? Are you serious?" but it's very real. It seems like being smart and being popular are polar opposites.

One young boy spoke up and said, "It is harder to be popular and intelligent. If the subject comes naturally, [...] it makes it easier. But if the subject doesn't come naturally, they work hard and other people see that and then you get the name-calling."

Basically, working hard meant that you would be teased. Girls also faced bullying for their efforts.

One young girl said, "My friends are all really nice people and have [a] really good sense of humor, and they're all really pretty and stuff, but because they do well in school they're not popular" (www.telegraph.co.uk).

The popular kids had very specific attributes, such as brand name clothing, and for girls, straight hair, and for boys, jelled up hair. But when it came to doing well in school, the boys who had the worst grades were generally thought of as the most popular.

CASE STUDY

Ben, 12 years old

Ben is in 7th grade. A classmate approached him — she was interested in dating him. He nicely said that he wasn't interested. It wasn't that he didn't like her; he just didn't want to date anyone. He was new to school and wanted to concentrate on his grades and getting a 4.0.

Next thing he knew, right before math class, he was being slapped in the face by the girl's best friend. Yes, this really happened.

You're Vulnerable

Sometimes people get made fun of because they're introverted (shy). They're looked at as "strange" or as "loners," because they often prefer to be alone.

That's a little crazy considering huge portions of the people in the world are introverted (it's estimated to be 33-50 percent).

If shyness sounds like a word that describes you, you might be getting bullied because of it. You're not alone — in fact, many people, including adults, talk about being looked at and treated differently for being shy.

Being an extrovert and having amazing social skills is looked at as the standard way of life — people think that's how you should be. Because of this idea, many people who are actually shy in nature pretend that they aren't so that they'll be accepted.

However, one introvert spoke up and wrote a book called "Quiet: The Power of Introverts in a World That Can't Stop Talking." That's right — a whole book was written talking about how awesome you and your quiet self are.

CLASSIFIED CASE STUDIES
directly from the experts

CASE STUDY

Amanda*, freshman in high school

Amanda explains her experience with bullying her first year of high school.

"I was really good friends with these girls going into high school, but as the year went on, they kind of stopped talking to me. They seemed to fit in more because they were more talkative. They raised their hand in class more and just talked more than me.

I felt left out. Sometimes they'd be whispering by me and I'd wonder if they were saying something about me.

Even things like hanging out after school set me apart. I'm really big on getting good grades and I wanted to do homework, but those girls just wanted to hang out."

Her mother says that Amanda is being really shy about just how bad things were. She explains what was really going on.

"Cell phones are allowed during lunch at her school, and she stopped taking bananas to lunch, because girls found it funny to take 'embarrassing photos' of people eating and then post them to Instagram.

Her school had an anti-bullying campaign, and the girls actually used the exact slogans and words to bully people. For example, the campaign posters would say, 'If you see a student that is alone, be friendly and say hello.'

The girls would say, 'Amanda! You are alone and look lonely! Hello!' They would walk away laughing. They couldn't be reported for bullying as they were doing exactly as was instructed by the anti-bullying campaign.

Amanda came home from school crying most nights."

*Name changed to preserve identity

You're Physically Different

Something about you is physically different than what everyone thinks is "normal."

You're tall, you're short, you're overweight, you're underweight, you have really bad acne, your ears stick out, your eyes are small, you have red hair, you wear glasses, you have a hearing aid, a lisp... the list goes on.

Something about you sticks out, and people are teasing you for it, probably coming up with some clever nickname, too.

This isn't some new thing, either. This has been going on for a really long time.

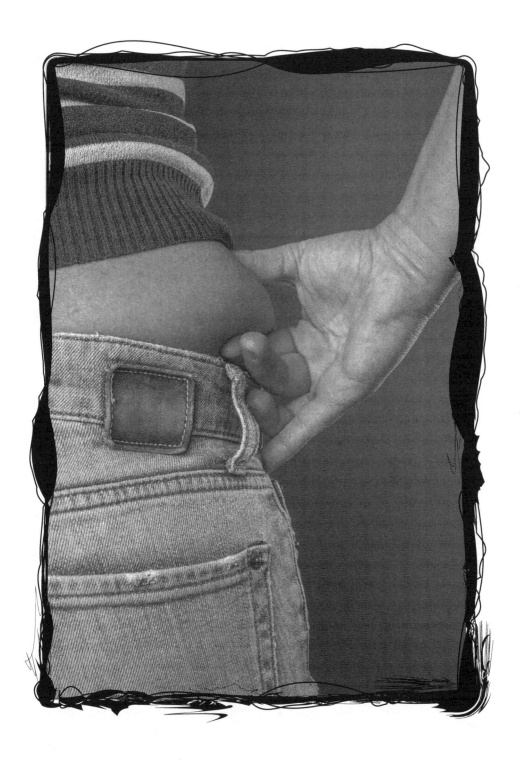

CASE STUDY

Heidi, 49 years old

"I'm 49 now. I'd say [the bullying] started in 6th grade. I had a 'boyfriend' in 5th grade that stopped talking to me and acted like I didn't exist when school started again in 6th. He became part of the 'popular' crowd, and I was left out. He literally pretended I wasn't there and never talked to me again. I was just starting to be heavier than the other girls at that point, not really fat, but not the super thin, which was really 'in' then. That would have been 1979. Things went downhill from there.

I hated school from that point on. I never had a good friend at school. My best friends were in my youth group at church, but not even one of them went to my school; they all were across town and went to a different high school. I didn't really have a good life until I married my husband.

It's amazing how our culture just doesn't 'see' overweight people."

You're in the LGBT Community

Being different when it comes to your sexual orientation is really difficult. Not only are you trying to figure out who you are, but you're probably also dealing with bullies.

You definitely aren't alone. Here are some facts about anti-gay bullying from Stomp Out Bullying™:

- 9 out of 10 LGBT students reported being harassed and bullied last year.
- Over one-third of LGBT students are physically assaulted at school.
- About two-thirds of LGBT students reported being sexually harassed.
- Over half of all students report hearing homophobic remarks often at school.
- More than 30 percent of LGBT students reported missing at least a day of school in the past month out of fear for their personal safety.
- The average GPA for students who were frequently physically harassed because of their sexual orientation was half a grade lower than that of other students.
- LGBT students are twice as likely to say that they are not planning on completing high school or going on to college.
- Gay teens are 8.4 times more likely to report having attempted suicide and 5.9 times more likely to report high levels of depression compared with peers from families that reported no or low levels of family rejection.

CASE STUDY

Jordan, 22 years old

"It all started when I was in 6th grade. It must have been the way I dressed. I was always well-dressed and never sagged my pants like all the other cool guys in the school.

In Oklahoma, the stigma of being a growing boy meant you played football. The only problem is, I never really cared for football.

The madness all started in the lunch café. Weaving through the crowd, I tried to find some nice people to sit with considering I had never been to this school before. Coming from central Illinois, it was a culture shock for me. I sat at the table that was considered the 'scene' table, which were teenagers that were decked in the latest gothic fashion and piercings — these were the only people who took me in.

Later during that week, I remember sitting at the table alone. I was first to get to lunch, and I was patiently waiting for my friends to join me. These two guys came over and sat right in front of me. I was quick to say hello but they just stared at me. They did not say one word but slowly stood up from the lunch table and started to rub their crotches in front of me, saying shockingly inappropriate things to me.

Ignoring them became more difficult as the weeks went by, but that was just the beginning of a very long and painful year."

You're a Minority

Being treated differently because you are a different race than someone else is not something that is only happening to people your age. It's happening everywhere and to everyone.

CASE STUDY

Anonymous, 8th grade through high school

"I was bullied from 8th grade to my freshman year, and every day they picked on me for my race," says a student that struggled with racial bullying.

"For a bit, one person made comments implying that I'm gay," he says. People teased him, calling him nicknames like "Ghandi" or other famous people that were the same race as him.

They singled him out in the locker room, made jokes about his skin color, and taunted him, calling him gay. He says he has no problem with people being gay, but he felt that the term was used to make fun of him just because he was physically different from everyone else.

"I feel that people most commonly use the words 'gay' or 'faggot' to describe people who are different from them and who they feel don't belong."

The worst part is that no one did anything. He later found out that his best friends were part of the bullying, secretly wishing that he would explode in anger at some point.

"There were so many silent witnesses who I wished would've spoken up or at least said something positive to me," he says.

He wants to use his negative experience to help other people and to give them a voice that he felt he didn't have: "all I want to do now is help others who are being bullied and prevent bullying from happening" (http://us.reachout.com).

You're Religious

The idea of being bullied for your religion dates back thousands of years. In fact, when Christianity was born, people were killed for it.

Being different in any way makes you an outcast in your classmate's eyes. Even your religion, which seems to have very little effect on other people, is a huge issue. Other people get really offended if you pray in public, for example.

Here's an example of a school that didn't really do anything to protect its Jewish students. (Hint: the school got sued.)

CASE STUDY

Anti-Semitic Bullying in New York

The NY Times reported that a New York school has to pay over four million dollars to settle a lawsuit against them.

The crime?

Jewish students were bullied in the school and no one did anything about it. These Jewish students said there were inappropriate drawings on the walls that made fun of them, they were given nicknames making of their religion, they were shoved and beaten, and worst of all, during bus rides, the other kids would have "white power" chants and would make Nazi salutes, completely terrifying them.

Apparently, the teachers didn't do anything about it. The bullying had a pretty bad effect on the students. The Times reports, "the students' grades had suffered, and they became withdrawn and depressed."

The student's complaints weren't taken seriously. When a parent emailed the superintendent about the problem, he responded by saying "I have said I will meet with your daughters, and I will, but your expectations for changing inbred prejudice may be a bit unrealistic" (www.nytimes.com).

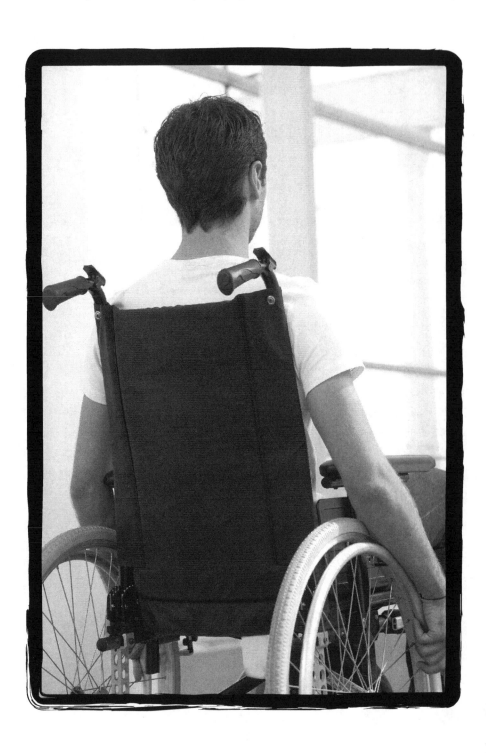

You're Disabled

If you're disabled, you're more likely to be bullied. That's just a fact. How much you are bullied depends on the type of disability you have, whether it be a specific learning disability, an emotional disturbance, other health impairments, a mild intellectual disability, autism, or a speech, hearing, or visual impairment.

A study done by George G. Bear and others from University of Delaware (2015) found that students with emotional disturbances were most likely to be bullied. Emotional disturbances means that the student has the following problems:

- Not able to learn effectively
- Not able to make healthy relationships
- Inappropriate behavior during normal situations
- Depressed moods
- Tendency to be schizophrenic

This doesn't limit bullying to people with emotional disturbances, though. Anyone who has a disability is at higher risk: "children with disabilities are generally at greater risk of bullying victimization than children without disabilities" (Bear).

Let's take a look at a real life story of a teen with Asperger's syndrome, which is when you have a hard time picking up on the normal social cues (among other things). Physically, these people look completely normal, but their behavior is different.

CASE STUDY

Michael, 15 years old with Asperger's Syndrome

"Growing up, people labeled me as an 'annoying freak with no friends.' And being the person I was, I couldn't figure out why. I told my parents every time it happened, but I never mentioned any specific names, because I was afraid that the kids doing it would get mad at me for reporting them.

In fourth grade, my parents decided to take me to a social specialist to figure out if I needed any specific help or if I had any form of autism. The results came back that I had Asperger's Syndrome. I never understood what it was until I started seeing a social worker in school.

I really realized that having Asperger's had been a problem for me in my life when I entered middle school. Kids around me wouldn't want to be around me, because I apparently annoyed them on purpose, which was a lie. They didn't understand that I had trouble understanding their social cues.

Almost every night I would cry myself to sleep, because I felt like I had no friends, that I was all alone in school with no one to talk to" (http://us.reachout.com).

Things did get better as the years went on. Michael realized that most of the kids treated him badly because they didn't want to be rejected. He talked to them one on one and things did resolve.

You're Poor (Or Too Rich)

Being in the wrong social class in school can put you at risk for being bullied and harassed. If you grow up in a school where being poor is the norm and your family has a lot of money, you might find that people start to make fun of you, simply because you're different.

On the other hand, if you grow up in a school where being middle class or rich is the norm, you're more likely to face some bullying, as well.

CASE STUDY

Jon, 35 years old

For Jon, the bullying started in the 4th grade, which was in 1991. He was new to the school, so he started out as an outsider.

He was very unpopular for a few reasons. He says he was short and skinny, and he was very poor. He lived in a trailer out in the country. Girls didn't pay him any attention, and he was the subject of a lot of harassment.

He explains that the bullying was a lot like what you see in TV: "People pushed me, they called me names like 'stupid' or 'poor boy,' and they knocked my books out of my hands."

However, he said it didn't really affect him. He had bigger problems going on at home. He did defend himself when he felt the need, though.

He got in trouble a lot for fighting back against the bullies. One day, on the school bus, Jon had enough and hit the bully back. The boy pinned his arm around and almost broke it, so Jon got free and punched him. A lot.

The bully never bothered him again.

You're a Girl

If you don't have enough factors working against you, you are more likely to be bullied if you're a girl.

Being a girl is stinkin' hard. In general, girls don't catch the headlines for violent rampages because of bullying, such as school shootings and serious assaults. Girls are also more likely to care about self-esteem and popularity rating. Because of this, a lot of researchers are really interested by the whole "mean girls" epidemic.

If you've ever heard that girls mature faster than boys, then you're right. By middle school, boys don't really care about popularity. It's not even on their radar. Girls on the other hand... well, girls are practically obsessed with it (in general).

The "popularity wars" among middle-school aged girls have an ironic twist: while boys are trying out their manhood on competitive sports, girls are vying for popularity within their own gender. In girl world, it goes without saying that the most popular girls will turn the heads (maybe) of the popular boys. Among girls, the popularity wars are internal (Perlstein 2004).

According to Rachael Simmons, author of *Odd Girl Out*, bullying by girls is not marked by the physical and verbal behavior that characterizes bullying by boys.

Girls do stuff like:

- Backbiting (talking about someone behind their back)
- Exclusion (you can't sit with us!)
- Spreading rumors (did you hear that...)
- Social scheming (pretending to like the fat girl so that you can make fun of her)
- Dirty looks (you know, the "glare")
- Being called sexually explicit names (such as "slut" or "ho")
- Being set up to look stupid (you don't know what that means?)
- Public humiliation (pulling your shorts down in gym class)

Does any of this sound familiar? Even if you're a guy reading this, you probably know what this is all about.

Well, the simple fact that you're a girl puts you at risk for being bullied. It's cruel, but it's true.

The worst part is that girls go for your soul. Guys usually throw a punch or an insult and get it over with. Girls, on the other hand, say things that hit you in the gut. They go for the silent, but deadly approach.

CASE STUDY

Marisa Simmons, 7th grader

Marisa Simmons had a great group of friends at her school, Griffith Middle School. They did everything together and they were really close. Marisa said one day the girls told her they were cutting themselves to feel better about the bad things going on at home.

She was worried about them and told her mother, who ended up telling the school principal. The next day, Marisa's friends were called into the principal's office, and when they came out, they looked at Marisa and knew she was the tattletale.

They turned on her.

They started spreading rumors about her, they called her explicit names, they told everyone she was pregnant, they said nasty things to her in the hallways, they posted mean things about her on social media... they were flat out mean girls.

Long story short, Marisa ended up switching schools. She is now much happier, but every time she sees a school bus go by, she ducks (www.nwitimes.com).

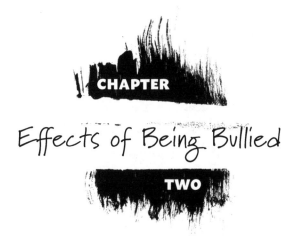

Effects of Being Bullied

Being bullied can have really profound effects on you and people your age.

McGrath lists off some possible outcomes:

- Increased illnesses, particularly stress-related illnesses
- Physical injuries resulting from being bullied
- Attempted and/or completed suicide
- Feelings of isolation, exclusion, and alienation
- Difficulty forming deep relationships
- Increased fear and anxiety
- Depression
- Feelings of incompetence and powerlessness
- Truancy (not going to school) to avoid the bully
- Increased absence from school due to stress-related illnesses
- Lower academic achievement and class participation
- Difficulty concentrating on schoolwork

If all of that isn't bad enough, you might start to have trouble sleeping because of the intense anxiety you're feeling.

Bullying may seem like something that will pass, and you can just move on from it, but it's not. It has the power to affect you right now as well as for the rest of your life. Read on to see some of the things that can happen because of bullying.

Chronic Trauma and PTSD

Unlike people who experience one bad thing one time, like a natural disaster, people who are bullied growing up experience chronic trauma.

People your age that experience chronic trauma are more likely, as adults, to develop addictions, compulsive behavior, depression, and anxiety.

If you're bullied, you're also more likely to develop Post-Traumatic Stress Disorder, or PTSD.

This disorder is really hard to live with, because it makes you feel really sad and angry all the time.

While that is a disorder that can develop over time, you're probably also wondering what bullying can do to you right now (which also really stinks).

Short-Term Effects

Bullying can make you feel lonely and unhappy. It can make you feel unsafe, both at school and at home, thanks to cyberbullying. You might start to feel like something is wrong with you (which isn't true; obviously you're awesome). You can start to have problems with self-esteem and anger, too. Worst of all, you can start to feel like the only way to survive all the bullying is to take your own life.

Memory Loss

When you're bullied really badly, your brain marks this is a stressful or traumatic event. Your brain wants to help you, so it blocks out those memories so that you don't have relive them (thanks a lot, brain).

This is actually called "dissociative amnesia." This basically means that you're brain is protecting you by burying the memories really deeply. You can't recall these memories on your own (**http://my.clevelandclinic.org**).

The only way to be able to dig up the traumatic memories is through a lot of counseling or by a trigger, which are most likely physical surroundings. For example, when you're old, you may decide to go back to your middle school and walk down the halls. You might suddenly remember something really stressful that you were unable to remember before.

This kind of memory loss happens more to women than men, and it's most closely linked to people who've been in wars. It sounds a little crazy to say that you could suffer from this condition just from bullying, but it's very possible.

In fact, it happened to me.

CASE STUDY

Rebekah, 21 years old

I transferred schools in the seventh grade. My parents couldn't afford the private school anymore, so I was an outsider to the public school. Everything was different. People were cursing in the hallways, people were talking about sex, and this one girl even got hit in the head by a lock (on purpose).

I tried to act like I fit in, but the truth was, I wasn't anything like these people. I did my best, and I actually made it into the "popular" group. Everything was going great. All the guys were writing me notes asking me to be their girlfriend — I think I was actually considered a popular girl.

But then, I dated one of the popular boys. You'd think this was the best thing ever, but things slowly spiraled. He lost interest and broke up with me. In the hallway. For everyone to hear.

He didn't even do it himself — he had one of his friends shout, "Rebekah. Andrew is breaking up with you. He doesn't like you anymore."

Suddenly, I was shunned from the popular group. Andrew didn't want anything to do with me, and all the popular kids were loyal to him over me. I had no one.

I wanted back in, so I tried apologizing to Andrew through a MySpace message (even though I didn't do anything), but he responded by telling me I was worthless and that I should kill myself.

The rest of the year is a blur. I don't really remember what happened in the rest of seventh or eighth grade. Sometimes, people will say, "Hey, do you remember when this happened?" And I'm shocked when I realize I have no idea what they're talking about.

In fact, when I think about those middle school years, it feels like I'm seeing a big, white, blank space. I can't remember anything.

By eighth grade, my parents realized that I couldn't take it anymore. I was begging to stay home, suffering from the physical effects of extreme stress, and one day, after a choir concert, one of the bullies told me he was going to kill me. My parents heard it, and they transferred me back to the private school overnight.

From that point forward, I remember a lot. But there's this one blank space that's really cloudy. I would give anything to get those memories back, but my brain has filed it all away in order to protect me.

Bad Grades

Bullying can actually cause your grades to suffer. Your GPA will start to fall and you won't be very good at those standardized tests. This is mostly due to your lack of concentration because of the bullying, as well as your likelihood to miss or skip school. (**http://www.stopbullying.gov**).

Violence

Being bullied so much can cause you to have a lot of feelings of built-up anger and resentment. It's possible that all of that can explode through violence.

There's the extreme of murder, which we'll see later on in this book with the Columbine shootings, but there's also much milder examples, like

punching someone. All of these negative effects of bullying sound about as good as moldy bread, if you ask me.

You need to know how to respond to the bullies; you need the tools to defend yourself so that you can avoid all of this stuff as best as you can (you can't control everyone, after all). Read on to learn some about some tools you can use to stop the bullies in their tracks.

CHAPTER

How to Defend Yourself Against Bullies

THREE

If you've ever been bullied, how have you responded? Some people respond by helping and encouraging the bully to target someone else. They do this in the hopes that the bully finds another, fresher victim. They feel like they'll finally be able to breathe a sigh of relief, knowing that the new toy will preoccupy the bully.

This is obviously not the way to go, no matter how much you think it will help you. Let's look at some of the best things you can do to defend yourself and keep that bully away from you.

Stop the Teasing

You have the ability to set boundaries. You can teach other people how to treat you.

In his book *Life Strategies*, Dr. Phillip C. McGraw writes that when we do not set limits assertively, we teach others that we can be manipulated, intimidated, and bullied.

If you're being teased and you don't set boundaries by letting the teaser know that the line between teasing and bullying has been crossed, you're teaching the bully that he or she can do or say anything to you. They aren't going to be afraid of any bad reactions, and they stop feeling bad about hurting you.

If you do this early on, you can prevent any future bullying. A simple "hey, I don't mind being teased every once in a while, but you're crossing the line," is a good way to stand up for yourself, and it lets the bully know that you are not to be messed with.

You'll be surprised by how much impact speaking up can have.

If you're not sure if you or someone else is being teased or bullied, here's a list that shows you the difference. This first list, "teasing," gives you an idea of the innocent nature of playful teasing.

- The teaser and the one being teased often swap roles with each other easily.
- Is not intended to hurt or humiliate the other person.
- Still maintains the dignity of all involved.
- Makes fun of someone in a lighthearted, clever, and benign way.
- Intended to make both parties laugh.
- Is but a small part of the activities of a peer group.
- Is innocent in motive.
- Is discontinued when the person who is being teased becomes upset with the teasing.

When teasing gets out of hand, there is a lot of apologizing going on. The teaser, who does not intend to harm a friend, backs off and respects the limits set in these interactions. The two friends are on an equal level of power and dominance. They like and respect each other and want to maintain their friendship.

- Is based upon an imbalance of power and is one-sided.
- Is intended to harm and humiliate.
- Is cruel, demeaning, and bigoted; thinly disguised as jokes.
- Encourages laughter at the victim rather than with the friend.
- Has the goal of diminishing the self-esteem of the target.
- Induces fear in the victim about further taunting and physical harm.
- Is sinister and mean-spirited in motive.
- Continues unabated despite the victim's distress or objection to the taunting.

There is nothing friendly or funny about a bully's taunts.

"Can't you take a joke?" says the bully with perfect innocence, leaving the impression that there is something wrong with you, not him. This is how the bully justifies his actions, and it's how he explains them to bystanders and adults if the bullying is discovered.

Just remember: you have the power to speak up, and now you have some knowledge to back up your side of the argument.

Speak Up

I know what you're thinking. If I tell my teacher or the principal, the bullying will get worse. And you may be right.

Let's weigh the pros and cons, though.

If you wait too long to let someone know that you're being bullied, you might be dealing with some of those effects mentioned above (not good). It's really common for the victim to keep everything to himself until he's about to explode. If you wait this long to try to get help, you're putting yourself at risk. By "at risk," this could mean you explode in anger (you try to get revenge through violence), or you explode by taking your own life.

By speaking up early on, you're not hanging off the cliff by a fingernail — you're slowly walking toward the cliff, if you know what I mean. You're protecting yourself.

Another thing about speaking up is that your teachers probably don't realize how bad the bullying is. It's not like bullies do their worst stuff in broad daylight — they do it when no one is looking. You'd be surprised at how much teachers do notice (they probably know you're texting under the desk), but they can't see everything.

Stop Cyberbulling

This may sound a little crazy, but being cyberbullied puts you at an advantage. The plus side to this kind of bullying is that you have evidence that you're being harassed. Anything that is said or posted online or to your phone can be copied and pasted and saved as proof that you're being bullied.

If you are being bullied online, take a screenshot or copy any kind of bullying that is happening to you. Then, block whoever is doing it.

Most importantly, *never* respond.

Once you do this, show your parents. If they think the bullying is bad enough, you can even get the police involved.

I don't think those bullies will be messing with you anymore.

Stop School Bus Bullying

Being bullied on the school bus is really common, because it's the perfect place for a bully to get away with it. The bus driver has to focus on the road, making it hard for her to see what might be going on at the back of the bus. Here are some things you can do if you're being bullied on the bus.

Sit as close as you can to the driver, and try to sit on the right side of the bus. This way, the driver can see you.

Pair up with someone, and ride the bus together.

Never fight back. Be polite. As much as you want to hock a loogie in their face, fight it. Kindness will throw the bully way off.

Tell an adult when it happens, especially the bus driver.

If you see someone else being bullied on the bus, stand up for them. Just asking them if they want to sit with you can be a huge help.

Don't Send Inappropriate Content

Most bullying is unavoidable. People will bully you for things you can't help, like being new or being poor.

However, one of the things you can control is what kind of content you're putting out there.

If you send your boyfriend a nude photo of yourself, you're putting yourself at risk. You may trust him, and he may have convinced you, but he can turn on you at any point. Also remember that if you're under 18, it's illegal.

Take this young lady, for example.

CLASSIFIED CASE STUDIES

directly from the experts

CASE STUDY

Jessica Logan, 18 years old

Jessica sent a nude photo of herself to her boyfriend. When they broke up, he sent the photos to a bunch of other girls. Those girls started to harass her at school, calling her names like "slut" or "whore."

Jessica started skipping school, because she was afraid of everyone.

Jessica decided to go on the news and talk about what was happening to her; she wanted to help anyone else who might be going through it.

Two months after she appeared on television, she hanged herself.

No picture is worth what Jessica went through. If it's possible to avoid that struggle between life and death, then do it.

Laugh at the Bully

This one may catch you off guard — and that's actually the point. You want to catch the bully off guard, too.

According to **www.stopbullying.gov**, this is something you should try if speaking up isn't working or if it's out of your comfort zone: "Try to laugh it off. This works best if joking is easy for you. It could catch the kid bullying you off guard."

By laughing, the bully realizes that your feelings aren't getting hurt. In fact, it makes it seem like you could care less. This might be just the thing you need to get the bully off your back.

Don't Play the Bully's Game

Bullies generally want three things from their victims to feel good about themselves: they want you to get upset, they want you to run away, and they want attention and power.

If you understand that this is the goal of their game, don't let them win!

Deny them all three of those things.

Act bored by sighing or yawning.

Don't run away from the bully. To make sure the bully isn't getting much attention and power, there are a few things you can do.

Avoid the Bully

If you know that the bully is at a certain place a lot, avoid it. If he stands by his locker between classes, don't walk past it.

Bullies thrive off of an audience, so if you do have to face him, do it at a time when not a lot of people are around. When you're face to face with someone, it takes the whole point of bullying away (and makes the bully feel a little more human).

Position Yourself

No, I don't mean throw up the knuckles and bend your knees. I mean position yourself in a stance of power.

There are a few ways you can stand that make the bully feel less powerful. One is to be looking down at him. If you can somehow make it so that you're taller than him, he'll feel less powerful. If he's sitting down, stand up. If you're on steps, make sure you're one step up.

By the way, never stare at the ground. Even if you can't make yourself higher, the worst thing you can do is to make yourself even lower. When you look down, it makes the bully feel even more powerful over you.

Another thing you can do is to walk, and look at the bully over your shoulder. It implies that you couldn't care less (which is the goal!). Just make sure that you don't run into the wall or something. That would really stink.

Speak Smartly

If you say anything at all, be sure to avoid the word "you" and any type of question. The goal is to make the bully feel like he or she doesn't matter to you at all.

By saying "you," you're acknowledging the bully's existence. By asking a question, you could be setting yourself up for failure. The bully could come back with a snide remark, making you feel even worse.

You also are showing the bully that you need something from him, which puts you in a weak position.

If you say anything, keep it short and insignificant. Phrases like "uh-huh" and "very clever" are good ones to use.

Whatever you do, don't join in on the game. If you insult the bully back, you're just as bad as he is.

Tell Someone You Trust

The best way to protect yourself from bullying is to talk to a parent or a teacher that you trust.

If you feel like you connect well with one of your teachers (or if they just seem really nice), tell them what's happening. Explain that you're being bullied, and be specific.

That way, they can keep an eye out for the bullying and can stop it when they see it.

Having someone who is there for you and that will support you is really important. Know that you aren't alone.

If no one seems to be doing anything, or they say something like "that's just how kids are," keep telling different adults.

According to Martin Cirkiel, a Texas lawyer who deals with bullying cases across the country, filing a lawsuit against a school district, teacher, or staff member can be hard, because various forms of immunity often protect them.

Sometimes adults have this mentality of "'boys will be boys.'" Martin goes on to say, "If a teacher or administrator learns that a student is being bullied and harassed, and they fail to correctly assess the situation and assure the necessary investigation is completed, they may open the school district and themselves to liability." In other words, you may come to a point where you can take them to court for not protecting you.

Being a girl is easier in this regard, because authorities take the complaints more seriously. If you are a boy, and your requests are being laughed at or are not taken seriously, know that you have legal rights, and you can use those to protect yourself.

Remind the adults that there are laws protecting you if someone is bullying you for your race, national origin, sex, disability, or religion.

Find the specific laws for your state at **www.stopbullying.gov/laws/ index.html**.

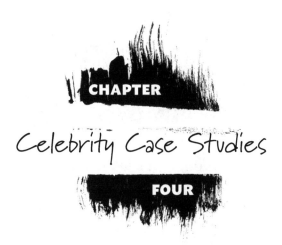

Celebrity Case Studies

CHAPTER FOUR

When we say that you aren't the only one being bullied, we really do mean it. Not only are kids across the country dealing with bullying, but those beautiful, famous people on TV dealt with it, too.

Read on to hear the bullying stories from some celebrities you might recognize.

Christina Aguilera

Christina Aguilera didn't fit in at school. Since a very young age, she has been in the spotlight as a performer, appearing on "Star Search" and "The Mickey Mouse Club." She says that many other children at school bullied her for her love of performing.

"I would get a lot of cold shoulders because there was just no way they could relate to what I loved to do," Aguilera said. "You know, it's not really normal for a child to just want to be in front of the camera and on stage... you know, it was hard for me to relate to other kids because I didn't have the same interests."

Does any of this sound familiar?

Aguilera said that the bullying became so extreme that someone slashed the tires on the family car, which led to her family moving. Eventually, Aguilera found a home with other young performers and became comfortable and confident in herself.

She has gone on to win five Grammy Awards and has sold more than 50 million albums worldwide. Now that she has found success, Aguilera has left her bullies far behind.

Michael Phelps

Before becoming arguably the greatest American Olympian of all time, even Michael Phelps struggled with bullying.

When he was a kid, Phelps was made fun of for his "sticky-out ears," his lisp, and his long arms (which turn out to be the perfect length for a swimmer). Like the superstar athlete that he is, Phelps took the taunts and used them as fuel.

American swimming coach Bob Bowman once said, "Michael is the motivation machine — bad moods, good moods, he channels everything for gain."

Phelps is so motivated that he has been known to even train on Christmas. Okay, you don't have to go *that* far.

He owns 18 gold medals (probably more ribbons than that bully got in track), which is double the second-highest amount ever. He also won 11 individual gold medals, and he is a testament to not letting bullying affect you. Instead, he channeled it in order to achieve greatness, which you can do, too.

Prince Harry

Even a crown cannot protect you from being bullied. Particularly in the case of Prince Harry, where the crown rests on a head full of red hair (we're looking at you, gingers).

As a "ginger" with colored hair and fair skin, Prince Harry was teased growing up. His army pals often called him the "Ginger Bullet Magnet" and joked that they would buy ginger wigs to wear in Iraq in order to keep insurgents from identifying him.

Prince Harry has not let his hair slow him down. He left the Army Air Corps in 2015 as a captain after 10 years of service with honorary military appointments in the Royal Navy and the Royal Air Force.

Take that, bullies.

Jessica Alba

When she was in school, Alba found herself among the uncool crowd. She had a Texan accent, buck teeth, and her family didn't have as much money as others in her class. Alba often spent her lunches in the nurses' office to find solitude and safety from her classmates. Her father would even walk her to school so she wouldn't be provoked.

Eventually, Alba turned to acting classes to channel her frustration and fear. She said that they changed everything for her. "The idea that for an hour I could be someone different was amazing," she said. "I was determined that this was something I was going to be good at. This was a part of my life no bully could ruin."

Alba has now appeared in more than 50 movies and television shows and received a nomination for a Golden Globe Award. She often encourages others to use their fear from being bullied as fuel to move forward. "You have to make it push you to become a stronger person, in whatever way that may be," she said.

Mila Kunis

You might have seen her in "That '70s Show," "The Book of Eli," "Black Swan," or "Oz the Great and Powerful." Mila Kunis is one of the most well known actresses in all of Hollywood. She's a powerhouse.

It wasn't always that way, though. She was made fun of in school for having a weird-looking face. Everyone made fun of her big eyes and her ears that stuck out funny. She came home crying after school some nights, desperately asking her parents why her eyes were so big.

Now, she's known as one of the most beautiful women alive. Sorry, what did you say, bully sir?

Famous actor, sold out shows, the host of the 2016 Oscars... Chris Rock is one of the most popular comedians in the world.

However, growing up, Chris had a really hard time. He grew up in the ghetto, and his parents wanted him to go a better school. They had him travel to a poor, white school, which made him one of the only black kids in his class. On top of that, he was also a skinny, short guy.

People constantly bullied him. They spit in his face, kicked him, and pushed him down stairs. Despite all of it, Chris says that he's glad he got bullied (um, what?). No, really, he's glad he was, because he said it helped him to think quickly on his feet, which is part of what has made him so successful as a comedian.

Jennifer Lawrence

If you didn't see her in "X-Men," you probably saw her in "The Hunger Games" or "Silver Linings Playbook."

When Jennifer was in elementary school, the mean girls bullied her. She switched schools a lot to get away from them. Then, in middle school, one of the mean girls gave her invitations to a party to hand out to all the other girls. She wasn't invited to that party.

"But that was fine," she says. "I just hocked a loogie on them and threw them in the trash can" (**http://pagesix.com**).

Jennifer was bullied by the mean girls, but that obviously didn't stop her. She's won an Academy Award and three Golden Globe Awards, she's done a huge ad campaign with Dior, and she's starred in some of the most popular movies to date.

Miley Cyrus

In Miley's book "Miley Cyrus: Miles to Go," she talks about being bullied in school. It started out pretty harmless, with just a girl rolling her eyes at a joke that Miley told. Then, she heard one of the girls snarl at her when she sat down for lunch: "I put my tray down at lunch and thought I heard a snarl. *A snarl?*" (2009).

Then, things got slightly worse, with one of the girls making fun of her clothing. It started to spiral, and Miley realized that the girls were turning on her. They started sending her mean notes, stole her books, made her late to class, and made fun of her clothes and hair. The girls even set her up so that she couldn't try out for the cheer-leading team.

Despite being bullied by all the girls, she went on to be the star of "Hannah Montana" and launched her singing career as a huge success (though we aren't sure what exactly happened after that).

Taylor Swift

The country turned pop music star was dumped by all of the popular girls in junior high.

You wouldn't think that one of the most successful music artists of the century was bullied in school, but it's true. The kids didn't think she was cool or pretty, and they made fun of her for liking country music.

Taylor says she probably wouldn't have been so motivated to write music if those girls hadn't been mean to her.

Another funny thing? When she scored her record deal in Nashville, she performed back in her hometown in front of all those mean girls. They came up to her with her T-shirt on asking her to sign their CDs. Times really do change, don't they?

Barack Obama

In case you still aren't convinced that you can be successful after being bullied, take a look at Mr. Prez.

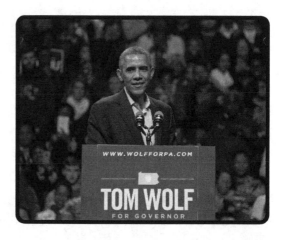

That's right, even the president of the United States was bullied in school. The kids made fun of his big ears and his strange name. The other kids taunted him, and he had to deal with the name calling every day.

He obviously went on to do great things, so if you feel like your life is over because you're being bullied, think again!

You See Bullying

People who watch bullying happen are silent witnesses. People even say that because these bystanders watch in silence, they're just as bad as the bullies.

If you've ever seen someone being bullied, what stopped you from speaking up? If you thought, "fear," that's a really common reason. You may have been afraid that if you report it, the bully will turn on you.

In this section, you're going to learn the role you play in bullying, how to react if you see someone being bullied, and finally, how you have the power to make a change in someone's life — because you do.

Your Role as a Bystander

You may not be the one being bullied, and you may not be the bully either. However, when bullying is happening, everyone plays a part, even the people on the sidelines.

If you see it happening, it's your job to stop it.

Bullying Myths

To understand your role better, here are some myths about bullying. You may think that bullying isn't happening at your school, but odds are, it is.

Bullying is everywhere, but not here

First, the myth that "We don't have bullies in our school" is just like denying that this behavior occurs daily in the United States and internationally. Studies show that it's happening — everywhere.

Teachers always stop bullying

Next, the myth that teachers and school administrators see bullying and stop it when it takes place is also incorrect.

Stories in the news of school shootings, such as Columbine, have shown that these kids were bullied, and teachers didn't do anything about it. You can't always rely on other people to stop the bullying.

In fact, you're the best one to do it, because the victim is your peer. Your words mean more to the bully than a teacher's words do.

Bullies are easy to pick out

Another myth is that bullies and bullying behavior are easy to see.

In reality, teachers and other adults may not realize that someone is being a bully. Bullies are rarely a social outcast, and they're usually clever enough never to allow an adult to see them doing the harassing.

It's your job to make sure that the adults know what's happening.

Bullies are big, ignorant males

The stereotype of a bully being male, ugly, mean-looking, big, clumsy, ignorant, and socially unskilled is not true.

The bully may be the captain of the football team, a member of the Honor Society, female, attractive, and/or socially outgoing.

Bullies can seem like really nice people, but the second the adults turn their backs, they can be vicious.

Make sure you're keeping your eye out for bullying. Don't assume that the bully is a certain stereotype.

Now that some common myths about bullying are debunked, let's take a look at what it really means to be a bystander.

Being a Hurtful Bystander

If you've seen or heard about someone being bullied, you are officially a bystander. You may think that since you aren't directly involved in the bullying, you are a neutral party.

The fact is, you rarely are. There a lot of things you might be doing as a bystander that cause more harm then good, which makes you a bully, too.

Laughing

If someone is being bullied, and you start laughing, you're being a hurtful bystander. The bully is thriving off of what everyone else thinks. When you laugh, you're encouraging the bully by giving him attention.

Instigating

If you see that the victim is in the prime spot or place to be bullied, and you say something to the bully, you're being a hurtful bystander.

For example, "Look at Ana. She has toilet paper on her foot. I dare you to go say something to her."

That is an example of instigating a bully. Remember to put yourself in someone else's shoes.

Passive acceptance

When you see bullying and don't do anything, you're passively accepting the fact that nothing is wrong with bullying.

This is almost as bad as laughing at the victim when he or she is being bullied. You're giving the bully an audience, which is what he needs to thrive, and you're also giving "silent acceptance," which is basically saying that you support what is happening (**www.eyesonbullying.org**).

Denying

One of the many reasons that bullying goes unreported by the victim is that his or her story can rarely be proven. The bully's bystanders deny that they witnessed any kind of bullying. The bully denies ever harming the victim. Only on rare occasions does an adult actually catch bullying occurring.

In 1993, Dr. Dan Olweus, the man who is considered to be the founding father of bullying research, found that, to keep from being discovered, much bullying occurred on the victim's way to and from school where no adults were observing. Again, the victim cannot convincingly report what nobody else saw.

Still, Olweus found that the overwhelming majority of bullying occurred on school grounds. The bully will say, "If you report me, no one will believe you, because no one saw it except the bystanders, who will lie for me."

In a crowded school, adults do not easily overhear threats, and what looks like bullying can be explained as an accident or just roughhousing.

The incidents that nobody saw and nobody heard are the bullying incidents that pass for something else. School officials, just like courts of law, tend to believe a story that can be *proven*, either by evidence or by eyewitness reports.

When the situation is a "he said, she said" kind of thing, the verdict goes to the bully. One incident of this sort will keep the victim, and other victims of bullying, from ever reporting it.

Why Bystanders Don't Act

If you've been bullied, and you've seen people watch, you may be wondering why no one is standing up for you.

The truth is, a lot of people *do* feel bad — you'll see in the next chapter the negative effects of being a hurtful bystander (you saw that right; being a bystander actually hurts you).

The problem is that there are a lot of things standing in the way between saying nothing and taking action.

The Bystander Effect

There is something that psychologists call "the bystander effect," which means that when there are a lot of people around, it discourages anyone from intervening in an emergency situation. This became a popular concept after the murder of Kitty Genovese in 1964, which we'll do a case study on later in this section (**www.psychologytoday.com**).

The main idea of this concept is that the more people there are, the less likely any one person will be to step up. Social thinker, Melissa Burkley Ph.D., explains how this is even a thing (2009).

First of all, a lot of bystanders don't realize that they're witnessing a crime. A lot of the time, people don't realize how serious a situation is, so they "look to others to see how they are reacting" (Burkley).

We've all done that in different situations, haven't we? It can be something as simple as seeing something funny in a movie — sometimes, we'll look around and see if other people thought it was funny, too. If they aren't laughing, sometimes we might stifle our own laughter so that we don't look crazy.

Here's another example that you might be used to: there's this math problem in class, and it's super confusing. You don't even know how to get past step one. The teacher is done explaining it, and your mind is super cloudy — um, what just happened? But before you raise your hand to ask for help, you look around the room. No one else seems to be confused. So, you don't raise your hand. You think you're the only one who doesn't get it, and you don't want to look stupid.

For the record, teachers find that if one student doesn't get the material, odds are most students don't. So, next time, raise your hand.

If everyone around isn't acting like there's an emergency, we don't realize the seriousness of the situation, so we don't do anything. In case you were wondering, psychologists refer to this as "pluralistic ignorance." Say *that* one five times fast.

The second big reason that bystanders don't do anything is something Burkley refers to as the "diffusion of responsibility." This is the idea that if a lot of people are seeing something horrible happen, they might not do anything, because they don't feel personally responsible. The more people there are, the less each person feels responsible. (There's 100 other people here; why do *I* have to do something if I'm only 1% responsible?)

The problem is that if everyone thinks like this (and the horror stories in the news suggest that most do), no one does anything at all.

The other crazy thing is that research shows that we don't think we're ignoring a bad situation because other people are around. Burkley talks about a study that was done using an intercom system.

Some of the participants took part in a one-on-one conversation over the intercom. The others took part in a group discussion with five other people. During the discussion, one of the voices on the intercom started having a seizure (it wasn't real, it was just a simulation).

Here's the real question — who intervened? Well, you might have a good idea.

The study shows that in the one-on-one conversation, 85% of the participants sought help. On the other hand, the group discussion showed that only 31% sought help. (Seriously?)

From an outside perspective, we can see clearly that having a group involved makes people seek help less. However, the participants didn't see it that way. The ones that didn't seek help said that they felt they weren't qualified enough to do anything. When the researchers asked if they didn't do something because other people were present, the participants said that had no affect.

Burkley says, "So even though the presence of others clearly affects our helping behavior, we are unaware of this influence."

Craziness!

Fear

As mentioned before, a lot of young people are afraid of getting hurt. They think that if they speak up, they'll be the new victims of the bully.

It's a selfish reason, but it's one of the most common ones.

Powerlessness

Another reason is because they feel like they don't have power. What if I say something to the bully, and he doesn't do anything?

Why would the bully listen to me?

This is another common reason, but a lot of people don't realize that, yes, in the moment, the bully may not listen to you. But, over time, your words will have an effect on the bully. Sometimes things just take time.

At a loss for words

We've all been tongue tied before.

Sometimes bystanders just don't know what to say without sounding stupid.

"Uh, excuse me, Mr. Bully. Can you, um, stop bullying?"

That's what these people imagine when they think about speaking up.

However, standing up for someone doesn't necessarily mean you have to say anything. Simply standing with the victim or touching their shoulder while the bullying is happening can show that you care, and it might be enough to make the bully feel bad.

If you're reading this and still don't feel like stepping in is something you can or should do, read on to understand how being a hurtful bystander can effect your future.

Effects on Bystanders

CHAPTER SIX

The whole point of being a bystander is staying away from bullying. You don't want anything to do with it, so you stand on the sidelines and watch. A lot of people like this think that it won't affect them at all — they think they're safe from the situation.

This is not the case. Bystanders suffer just like the people who are actually bullied.

Drug and Alcohol Abuse

Kids who watch other people get bullied are more likely to get into drugs and alcohol. This isn't temporary, either. Drug and alcohol abuse can extend into adulthood.

Bystanders can feel shame, guilt, and regret from not doing anything, which leads them to substance abuse to dull the pain. It doesn't do much except provide a temporary release from the pain. In the long run, it actually makes things worse.

Mental Health Problems

Mental health problems such as depression and anxiety are more likely to increase if you're a bystander.

Not taking action to help someone else can affect your brain by building up those feelings of regret, which can then manifest itself into actual conditions, such as depression.

Skipping School

If you don't take action for someone else, you're more likely to miss or skip school.

You may not want to put yourself in that position, thus avoiding even being a bystander. By completely staying away from the bullying, you allow yourself to avoid any kind of responsibility. This can hurt your grades.

Bullying, in general, has a lot of negative effects on everyone, including the bullied, the bystanders, and the bullies, which we'll cover in the next section.

Keep on reading to learn how you can make a change and avoid all of the negative effects that bullying can have.

CHAPTER

Making a Change

SEVEN

Studies show that the bully needs an audience. According to Emily Bazelon (2014), author of "Sticks and Stones," for every ten instances of bullying, nine of them have a significant audience, and only 20 percent of the bystanders intervene (108).

That means that for every five times someone is bullied, the victim is only defended once.

You may be timid or shy, which means that stepping in and defending someone else is out of your comfort zone.

However, when you look at the negative outcomes that being a bystander can have on you, and when you pair that with the crushing effects that being bullied can have on the victim, you know that it's your duty to do something.

Let's look at some of the things you can do to help stop bullying.

Be a Friend

You don't have to hang out with the kid that gets bullied everyday. I mean, you can if you want to go above and beyond, but you don't have to.

Something as simple as a kind word (and I mean a genuine, kind word) can make someone's day.

Being nice to the bullied kid is one of the best things you can do to make a change. Saying "hello" when you see them and asking them what they thought of that really hard test in physics is all it takes.

Include the Victim

Sit with the kid at lunch; sit with him on the bus. If you're doing a group project, make sure you're keeping that person in the loop.

If you're having a birthday party, invite the victim.

Make sure you aren't leaving that person out on purpose. If you are, that makes you a bully, too.

Tell an Adult

If you're too afraid to do something in the moment, find an adult and tell them what's happening.

Again, make sure it's someone you trust. If there's a teacher or administrator who seems like they hate their job or could really care less, they might be the best person to tell. Not every adult knows how to handle situations like this.

If you do tell an adult, and they don't do anything, tell another. Keep asking for help until someone steps in. Don't give up until you know you're making a change.

Suggest Change

Sometimes, adults need a kick in the butt. Maybe they don't realize that bullying is such a problem.

If you really want to make a change in your school, suggest it.

Talk to your principal or teachers about having a school-wide presentation.

Start an anti-bullying petition. Send it around at your school, and have everyone sign it.

Tell your principal that National Bullying Prevention Month is in October. Ask him to honor it by doing something to raise awareness.

Let the adults know that there is a problem, and that there are steps you, as a school, can take to make a difference.

Start a Campaign

You might be thinking that this is out of your reach, but it isn't. There are a lot of organizations out there that have everything all set up for you — all you have to do is raise a little money and ask your principal to hold a school-wide assembly.

Biggest. Assembly. Ever.

The deodorant brand, Secret, hosts a live stream every year about bullying (yes, you heard that right).

The event is hosted by Keenan West and features a lot of guest appearances (lots of celebrities!).

The goal of this event is to teach everyone what bullying looks like, how to handle it, and how to eventually stop it.

The concept of live stream is that you use the Internet to project the event on a big wall or a screen, kind of like Skype. It's live, though, so it's not like you're just watching a movie or a video. It's actually happening as you're sitting and watching. They do it every February.

You can sign your school up at **http://meanstinks.com/rsvp**.

In addition to this big event, the website made by Secret, called Mean Stinks, has lots of helpful tools and information that you can use. Girls talk about their experiences with bullying, and there are posters that you can download and print to hang up in your school.

There's also a competition for "Nicest School in America" where schools create a "Wall of Nice" mural and submit it to the contest. This is a great way to get everyone involved (and have a little creative fun, too).

Pacer: You're Not Alone

The Pacer website, found at **www.pacer.org/bullying/getinvolved**, is a great campaign option. It's really affordable, too — around a dollar per person. There are a lot of things that this site has to offer, including a campaign called "You're Not Alone."

The concept of this campaign is to create a community. Educate people who don't know there is a problem, and let the people who feel alone know that they aren't.

With this campaign, you have two options. You can have a classroom activity, which costs 50 cents per person, or you can hold an event, which costs $1.50 per person.

Classroom activity

The goal of the classroom activity is educate students on how to help victims and also to let victims know that they have people that support them.

This toolkit is meant to inspire students by creating a place where they can actually talk about these problems. The kit comes with posters, stickers, and handouts.

Hold an event

The goal of this is the same as the classroom activity, but it's on a bigger scale. It adds a sense of seriousness to it, because everyone is involved. It's more of an actual occasion — something that everyone is talking about.

This kit comes with posters, buttons, handouts, shoelaces (meant to help kids feel unified if they're all wearing the orange shoelaces), a pledge, flyers, and bookmarks.

If you aren't sure how to raise the money for a program like this, the Pacer website has a lot of good ideas, such as having a pajama day where you donate money to the cause for the right to wear pajamas, or hosting a sporting event. To see more ideas, visit **www.pacer.org/bullying/getinvolved/fundraising-ideas.asp**.

Bullying. No Way!

This is a popular anti-bullying website based out of Australia that has a lot of ideas on how to raise awareness.

Here are a select few:

- Hold an anti-bullying poster design or other artwork competition — involve members of the broader community to present prizes.
- Organize a free dress day with a special feature (such as wearing odd socks or a single color) that symbolizes inclusion and diversity in your school community.
- Plan for a series of anti-bullying assemblies in the week leading up to the National Bullying Awareness Day. Different groups of students could lead the assembly each day.
- Highlight your anti-bullying policy on your school's website.
- Make a school mural of positive messages about students' contribution to making your school safe and supportive.

While bullying is a problem year-round, these are some really great ideas to use during National Bullying Awareness Month. Your school administrators are more likely to get excited about something like this because of the special time of year.

Treat this time like you would Homecoming week. Plan something special each day of the week leading up to a big assembly or event on Friday. Take the lead — this kind of initiative is something that will not only make you feel like you're making a difference, but it'll also look good on that résumé of yours (double duty!).

To read more campaign ideas, visit **http://bullyingnoway.gov.au/ national-day/for-schools/school-events.html**.

STOMP Out Bullying™

This is another organization with the goal of helping to stop bullying. They have several different campaigns that are designed to draw awareness to the issue.

Blue Shirt Day®

This is an event held on the first Monday of each October. STOMP Out Bullying designs the blue shirts, and to participate in this annual event, you have to fill out the form (**www.stompoutbullying.org/index.php/campaigns/want -participate-blue-shirt-day-world-day-bullying-prevention**).

NO MATTER!™

STOMP Out Bullying also has a campaign called NO MATTER! that is designed to draw attention to the fact that we're all different. The only thing you have to do to participate in this campaign is to share it to your social media by visiting (**www.stompoutbullying.org/ index.php/campaigns/no-matter-campaign**).

National Bullying Prevention Awareness Month

STOMP Out Bullying also has a lot of ideas on things you can do during the month of October in addition to Blue Shirt Day.

The week of October 12th is designated as "make friends with someone you don't know at school" week.

The week of October 19th is "STAND UP for others" week.

The week of October 26th is the participation week, which asks that you do one of the following things:

- Create positive messages on sticky notes, and hand them out to students at school.
- Create anti-bullying videos and share them on the STOMP Out Bullying site.
- Share inspirational stories on the STOMP Out Bullying site.
- Create an act of kindness every day and challenge others to do the same. Make kindness go viral!

Kognito Online Simuations

If you feel like an assembly is too out of reach, talk to your school staff about holding an online class about bullying. It's less of a class and more like a game. It's a simulation with a real-looking environment (like a classroom). You can practice conversations with emotionally responsive virtual people. Yes, it's as cool as it sounds.

As you go through the course, you learn how to better handle actual situations. What's the right thing to say when my friend says she's going to come out to her parents? How do I handle a situation where I'm a bystander to someone being bullied?

The goal of these short courses is to help you learn what to say and when to say it. The program is usually paid for by the school's government funds, often times grants. It costs about $30 per person, but a spokesperson for the company said that price is significantly reduced when an entire school signs up.

Consider bringing this up to your principal, and ask if it's something that he or she would consider doing. For more information, visit **www.kognito.com**.

Famous Case Studies

EIGHT

Being a bystander can change a life. That's why there are as many news stories about bystanders as there are about bullies and their victims. The sad part? Most of them are about people seeing something horrible happening, and then not doing anything about it (remember the bystander effect?).

In this chapter, we'll take a look at some horrific examples of bystander stories, and then one case of a helpful bystander.

The Holocaust (1933–1945)

The Holocaust? Really? Yes.

The Holocaust is probably the most famous case of the hurtful bystander. And hurtful is most definitely an understatement.

If you're not too familiar with what the Holocaust is, I'll give you a short introduction. The Holocaust was the Hitler-endorsed murder of around six million Jews. The word "Holocaust" means "sacrifice by

Auschwitz Camp

fire." A lot of the Jews were put into what looked like huge showers just to be burned alive.

The murder of the Jews was thought by the Nazis to be a social cleansing. They were committing "genocide," which means killing a specific group of people on purpose.

The Jews were completely innocent — they hadn't done anything wrong. I know it sounds crazy that something like this could actually happen (are people that crazy?), and the scary thing is that it wasn't really that long ago. Your grandparents were probably around when this happened.

Anyway, to get back to the point, the Nazis were bystanders. It may seem more appropriate to call them bullies, but in reality, most of them

ADOLF HITLER
© GLOBE PHOTOS, INC.

were just watching and following along. A lot of them said, "we were just following orders."

The Nazis claimed that they were surrounded by Germans (their people), which meant that if they tried to report what was going on to the outside world, they would've been killed. This was truly a situation of life or death.

Beyond the actual Nazis being bystanders (and often bullies), the surrounding towns also didn't do anything. People could smell the burning bodies from 20 miles out, and the people in those cities and towns didn't do a single thing.

When the Allies (the countries that stepped in to stop what was happening) won the war, they accused these passive people of knowing

what was going on and not doing anything about it. As punishment, they were forced to clean up the bodies and bury them in huge graves.

Richmond High School Incident (2009)

Here's another case of the hurtful bystander. A 15-year-old girl went to her homecoming dance, probably expecting to drink some punch and dance to corny dance music.

However, her night ended up being a horror story. She was gang raped (sexually assaulted by many people). It is suspected that around 20 people were involved in the incident.

It happened in a back alley at the school. They think that about 10 people were actually assaulting her, while the other 10 or so were watching and not doing anything about it.

When the young girl was found, she was unconscious underneath a bench. She was flown to a hospital in critical condition.

The most disgusting part of this whole thing is that when people heard what was going on, they showed up to watch, and sometimes even joined in. (Information courtesy a CNN news report.)

The Murder of Kitty Genovese (1964)

This is the story of a woman who was killed outside of her apartment in Queens, New York City.

The 1964 NY Times article says that 38 people watched the killer "stalk and stab a woman in three separate attacks" without doing anything.

No one called the police, let alone intervened. Twice, the sound of the bystanders' voices interrupted the killer and made him back off. But every time he came back, he found her and tried to kill her again. When Kitty died, one person called the police. By then, it was too late to save her.

Everyone heard her screaming, "Oh, my God, he stabbed me! Please help me! Please help me!" but the only thing that anyone did was to yell back down from the window, "Let that girl alone!"

The police said that the killer took around 35 minutes to kill her. If the police had been called, she would still be alive.

The Eagle Buddies (2006)

Being a bystander doesn't just mean that you're standing there watching the bullying. It means that you hear about the bullying going on.

When a five-year-old was being bullied at school, some football players heard about it and decided to do something (take notes!).

Chris Kuykendall and Brevin Young, Hobbs Eagle football players, heard that a five-year-old boy at his school, Ryan, was being bullied.

"It was heartbreaking to know a kindergartener was going through something like that," Chris said on the Meredith Vieira show.

The young boy was throwing up before school because he dreaded being bullied. Other boys would trip him, kick him, and punch him. When Meredith asked him if he ever told the boys to stop, he said, "No, I couldn't, because if I did, they'd just say, 'no, you're not my boss!'" He also said that one of his friends tried to stand up for him, but it backfired, because he ended up getting bullied, too.

Chris said he was bullied as a young boy, too, so he felt like it was his mission to do something about it.

Chris decided to sit with the boy during lunch where everyone would see them.

"When you see a football player from afar, you say wow," Chris says, "You see me eating with him and all the kids say 'wow, he must be really cool if a football player is sitting with him.'"

Ryan started doing a lot better — he stopped throwing up, started playing on the playground, and his mood changed drastically. He said in tears, "I know that they'll stop the bullying."

When the rest of the football players saw what was happening, they knew they had to join in. All of the football players would eat lunch with the bullied kids, and it made a huge difference.

This is now called the Eagle Buddies Lunch Program.

You're a Bully

This section isn't just directed at actual bullies (um, I'm not a bully!), though it can be (am I a bully?). The main purpose of this section is to help you understand why bullies are... well, why they're bullies. What motivates them, why are they so mean, and most importantly, why do they feel the need to pick on you?

If you can understand these things, dealing with the bully will be a lot easier. It will change your perspective about them and help you to realize that, in the end, we're all humans.

As a quick initial overview, let's take a look at the different types of bullies, courtesy Barbara Coloroso (2003).

The confident bully

The confident bully has a big ego, but not a strong one. This type of bully has an inflated sense of self, a sense of entitlement, a liking for violence, and has no empathy for those he hurts. This bully only feels important when inflicting pain upon others. He has a powerful, overwhelming personality and feels superior to others.

The social bully

The social bully prefers rumor, gossip, verbal taunts and shunning, isolating the victim, and excluding her from school activities. She has a poor sense of self and hides her insecurities in a cloak of charm and exaggerated confidence.

The fully armored bully

This bully comes across to others as being cool and detached. He shows little emotion. He looks for opportunities to bully when he cannot be seen and caught. He is cruel and vicious to his target, but charming in front of others.

The hyperactive bully

The hyperactive bully struggles with his schoolwork and has poor social skills, because he does not process social cues accurately; he perceives that others want to harm him and reacts aggressively to these non-existent cues: "I'll get them before they get me."

The bunch of bullies

This is a group of friends who, together, do things that they would not do if they were alone. Their goal is to isolate, exclude, and scapegoat their target.

The gang of bullies

This gang forms not out of friendship but as a strategic alliance that pursues power, control, and domination over others. Drawn together, they bully others to gain respect from their gang, and lack empathy and remorse for their actions.

The bullied bully

This type of bully is both a target and a bully. She is bullied by older kids and by adults; she bullies others of her same-age or younger peer group to feel relief from her sense of powerlessness and self-hatred. This kind of bully is sometimes referred to as a bully/victim.

Okay, so you're familiar with the different kinds of bullies. If you've ever wondered "why do they do it?" or "am I a bully and don't even know it?" then keep on reading.

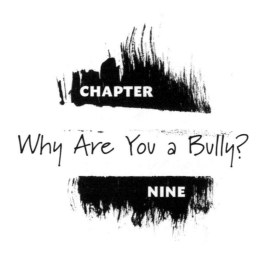

Why Are You a Bully?

CHAPTER NINE

So, why? Why do classmates feel the need to physically and emotionally hurt other people?

Well, there are a lot of people out there wondering the same thing. Many different organizations have done studies and tests and have tried to come up with a good answer. Let's look at what they've come up with.

Mental Illness

Have you ever heard of something called the "insanity defense?"

Let's say someone kills someone else. They have the right, in court, to claim that they're insane. If they claim this, and it's found to be true, they are excused of their actions and are found to be not responsible. Then, the person is most likely forced to see a psychiatrist, and they have to go through some kind of treatment in a mental institution.

Now, think of this concept in terms of bullies.

To some, this seems like a cop out. It's way of justifying the actions of the bully. "Well, that poor kid has a mental illness — he didn't know what he was doing." To others, it seems like a way to explain the bully's behavior, but to not excuse the bully from personal responsibility.

According to the biggest book ever — okay, maybe not *ever* — there's a condition called "conduct disorder." This basically describes bullying.

According to the DSM-IV-TR, this is a disorder young people have that causes the following problems:

- Aggression to people and animals including bullying, threatening, or intimidating others
- Destruction of property
- Deceitfulness or theft
- Serious violations of rules at home, in school, and in society as a whole

The DSM-IV-TR says that kids with this condition come from homes where there is domestic violence, substance abuse, criminality, poverty, and neglectful, uninvolved parenting.

When you grow up in a home like this, it's really hard for a kid to feel bad for other people, and it's also really hard for that same kid to create relationships. This is the perfect environment to create a bully.

This condition is only for young adults, though. Once you turn 18, you graduate to the big stuff, something called Anti-Social Personality Disorder, or ASPD. This is a really serious condition — these kinds of people have absolutely no remorse or sympathy for people they hurt.

They're really good at manipulating and intimidating people so that they get what they want.

That horrible list of things on the last page suddenly turns into something pretty freaky. People with ASPD:

- Frequently engage in criminal behavior, including homicide (murder)
- Will not conform to social rules, laws, or norms
- Are impulsive and do not learn from their mistakes
- Have no sense of responsibility
- Have irritable, angry, aggressive thoughts and feelings
- Are often involved in physical fights with no regard for their safety or the safety of others

That bully at school may not have these disorders, but if they do, you now know and understand that it isn't you with the problem — it's them.

A "Disconnect" in Childhood Development

It's possible that there was a kind of mis-fire in the bully's childhood development. A "disconnect" occurs in the bully's brain when they're growing up. They don't really understand how to feel bad for someone, and they don't realize when they're causing harm.

When the bully acts out by being violent or aggressive, it might be because of their development.

With this, there's kind of a timeline that can help us understand where the bully was born.

In early childhood, the bully's parents didn't really discipline him. They let him do just about anything, and they didn't pay him much attention (which is every kid's dream, right?).

In middle childhood, the bully is rejected by "normal" peers because he's a bit aggressive and isn't really good at school.

In late childhood and early adolescence, the bully starts to do "bully-ish" things like exploiting people and making fun of them.

At this point, the bully is truly born.

Once the bully is born, it's really hard to turn back time and change him. There are bullies out there that appear to have a lot of friends, but it's because people realize that if they don't like the bully, they might become the one who's made fun of.

Bullies for Parents

Children learn through imitation. If you ever interact with a baby or a toddler, you'll notice that she imitates just about everything you say or do.

With that in mind, it makes sense that kids also learn to be bullies if their parents are that way.

If parents don't handle conflict well or are violent, it's more likely that their children will be the same way (**www.stompoutbullying.org**).

This also goes for siblings — if the child's brother or sister is a bully, it's more likely that the kid will turn into a bully, too.

In general, studies show that kids who are bullied are more likely to become bullies themselves, so maybe that bully isn't as cold-hearted as we originally thought.

Craving Power and Attention

It's possible that the bully isn't getting any attention at home, so they try to get it at school. Being powerful is a way of getting attention.

To be powerful, bullies target people who look weak, and they suck the life out of them. They do this by manipulating them, gossiping, and just being flat out mean.

A lot of bullies also just don't realize what they're doing. They focus on the fact that they're getting attention and power instead of how it's making the other person feel. Bullies are really bad at putting themselves in other people's shoes.

Stomp Out Bullying talked to some bullies to try to understand why they are the way they are. Here are their responses:

- Because it makes me feel stronger, smarter, or better than the person I'm bullying
- Because I'm bullied at home
- Because it's what you do if you want to hang out with the right crowd
- Because I see others doing it
- Because I'm jealous of the other person
- Because it's one of the best ways to keep others from bullying me

It might seem really, *really* hard to sympathize with a bully, but by understanding their history and where they're coming from, it can help you as a victim. You gain a new perspective — the bully is suffering with his or her own problems and is taking that out on you.

Whenever you see someone being a bully, try to think about what they might be experiencing. Maybe they have a really bad home life, or their parents are violent. Try to understand why they are the way they are — it will help you realize that the bullying isn't about you at all. It's about the bully and his or her weaknesses.

By sympathizing with the bully, you're taking a step forward and doing one of the hardest things you can do as a human being — you're loving your enemy.

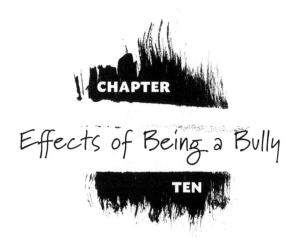

Effects of Being a Bully

Being a bully seems to have obvious effects (of course the bully is cold-hearted and mean). However, the effects of being a bully stretch out a lot. Bullies are more likely to suffer from some pretty big problems for the rest of their lives.

If they are allowed to bully in school and get away with it, they will go on to be workplace bullies. Randel notes that bullies tend to have less education, a higher dropout rate, and more unemployment.

Bullies are also at greater risk of suicide than their victims.

In general, bullies are risk-takers and start to care less and less about other people.

Violence

Bullies are more likely, in general, to be violent. They're more likely to get in fights with other people, and they're also more likely to vandalize property.

Relationships are more likely to suffer. Bullies have a higher tendency to be abusive towards people in their life, including their partner and their children.

Bullies have a higher tendency to become involved in youth gangs, as well.

Bullies are more likely to have criminal convictions (ending up in jail or prison) as well as traffic citations (like speeding tickets). They're generally more likely to disobey the law.

According to Derek Randel (2006), author of "Stopping School Violence," bullies identified by age eight are six times more likely to be convicted of a crime by age 24 than non-bullies.

In 2003, Fight Crime: Invest in Kids conducted a study on bullying. Nearly 60 percent of the boys who researchers classified as bullies in grades six through nine were convicted of at least one crime by the age of 24. 40 percent of them had three or more convictions by 24, the report said.

In another study that spanned 35 years, researcher E. Eron followed several children from the age of eight who were identified as bullies by other children (qtd. in Garrett, p. 75). The result of Eron's research is not surprising; he found that childhood bullies continued to bully as adults.

They required more governmental aid because of their tendency to end up in jail. They had higher rates of alcoholism requiring government-subsidized treatment, and their development of personality disorders caused them to have multiple, unstable, and violent marriages.

They spent a lot of time in court.

Mental Health

A team of researchers came together and did a really huge study on teenagers. They wanted to find out if bullies ended up having more mental health problems then non-bullies.

They did some tests when the bullies were 14-15 years old and again when they were 27. You'll never guess what they found. (By the heading, I think we both have an idea.)

Yes, they were found to have more mental health problems. This study was published in Child & Adolescent Psychiatry & Mental Health (2015). It found that those being bullied *and* the ones doing the bullying were more likely to end up in the hospital for mental health problems like depression (11). Victims and bullies are also more likely to internalize problems.

This was a study done on real people like you — it isn't just some made up statistic. These people actually ended up in the hospital a decade later because of some stuff that happened in middle school and high school.

Another study (2014) found that bullies are "impulsive and aggressive toward their environment" (Horrevorts 770). Bullies are more likely to have conduct disorder (remember that condition that bullies are sometimes diagnosed with?). The study even says that bullies are more sensitive to "developing psychotic phenomena, like sub-clinical psychotic experiences" (770).

Psychotic experiences do not sound the least bit enjoyable.

Education

Bullies are more likely to do worse in school, too. A study done by another group of researchers that was published in the Journal of Youth and Adolescence (2013) found that bullies and bully/victims (kids that were once bullied and then turned into bullies) have more academic problems.

They're more likely to skip school and do poorly in class (Bradshaw). The study even says that the academic problem is just "'the tip of the iceburg,'" and that these students are experiencing a lot of other problems, like drug and alcohol abuse and involvement in gangs.

So, what can we do to stop the bullies?

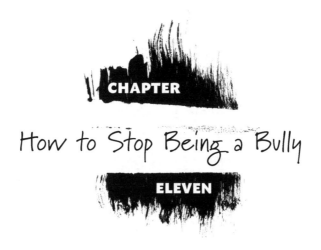

How to Stop Being a Bully

CHAPTER ELEVEN

If you realize that you have a tendency to bully other people and want to take the steps to stop, here are some things that can help you, courtesy **www.ditchthelabel.org**.

Keep in mind that being a bully doesn't necessarily mean that you beat up other people or that everyone thinks of you as the bully. Something as simple as gossiping about other people or making fun of them is bullying, too.

Increase Your Emotional Intelligence

Jarvis Howe, M.A., a clinical psychologist, explains that if you can learn how to manage your emotions better, you're less likely to bully other people. He even says that it can help you deal with anxiety, which can explain why you lash out on other, innocent people.

Emotional intelligence just means that you can recognize the meanings of emotions (ever seen the movie "Inside Out?"), which helps you to be a better problem solver. If you're smart about emotions, you can use that information to help you think and behave better.

If you are curious about your emotional intelligence, you can take a quick EQ quiz at **www.ihhp.com/free-eq-quiz**, **http://personality-testing.info/tests/EI.php**, or **www.queendom.com/ tests/access_page/index.htm?idRegTest=3037**.

Ditch Labels

When you label yourself, you're hurting your self-esteem. If you think of yourself as a "bully," you're putting limits to the fact that you can change.

Bullying is something we do; it's an action, not a label. You are a human that bullies. Not a bully.

Do not self identify with the term "bully." Remember that you are an individual, and you have the power to turn your behavior around.

Remind Yourself Why

After reading all the reasons why you might have a higher tendency to bully other people, take it heart. Know that other factors have affected you, whether it is your home life, a stressful situation, or even feelings of jealousy.

Understanding who you are and what you've been through that has gotten you to this point is the key to being able to stop.

When you have the urge to bully someone, remind yourself of these things.

For example, "Yes, my father bullied me, and my mother never paid attention to me, but I am bigger than my upbringing. I am bigger than this."

See a Counselor

If you have been able to figure out what has caused you to want to bully others, then you're already on the right track. Being able to talk to someone else who has some real education and knowledge on the subject can help you in a big way.

If you aren't able to figure out where these hateful feelings are coming from, a counselor or therapist can be a huge help. Sometimes you need an outside perspective to open your eyes.

A lot of the time, there is a school counselor that you can see for free. If not, ask your parents or a teacher what your options are. If you don't think either of these things are an option, consider looking at the website **www.childline.org.uk**. You can join a waiting room where you can actually talk to a counselor.

The only downside to the online chat room is that the counselor can't see your body language, and they can't hear your tone of voice. Professionals are trained to pick up cues from you, and if they can't see or hear them, they're limited in how much they can actually help you.

Relieve Your Stress

Stress can make people do all kinds of things, including lashing out on others. (It can also make you sweat more in case you were wondering.) Not only is a bully most likely feeling stress, but the victim is, too.

There are some things you can do to relieve your stress in a healthy way. Try doing these things, and see if it changes your mood.

Breathing

Yes, yes, I know you breathe all the time, but to help get rid of stress, try breathing more deeply. Take a minute or two, close your eyes, and breathe.

The goal of breathing deeply is to have your stomach rise up and down, not your chest. Breathe as slowly as you can. You'll be surprised at how just a few, concentrated, deep breaths a day can impact your mood.

Listen to music

I know you do this already, but turn off the screamo and the old-school hip-hop for just a minute. Spas play relaxing music for a reason — it actually reduces your stress. By listening to soothing music both before you go to sleep and when you wake up, you can help your stress levels fall.

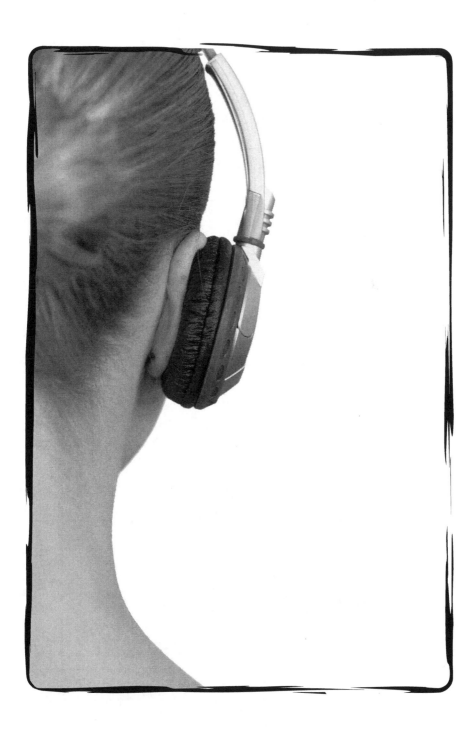

Laugh

This list seems a little weird, I know, but I promise these things actually do make a difference. Watch a funny movie or listen to a funny comedy clip. According to WebMD (2015), "laughing first activates and then relieves your stress response, producing an overall feeling of calm. A good belly laugh also improves the body's oxygen flow and blood circulation, and it can do wonders to improve your attitude."

Even if nothing is funny, try just sitting there and fake laughing. Your brain doesn't really know when your laugh is genuine and when it isn't — it will still activate and relieve your stress response, so you may look kind of strange, but you'll feel better.

Exercise

You can do any kind of exercise you want. You can run, play tennis, do kickboxing, and go swimming; you can do just about anything you like to do that causes you to sweat.

When you exercise, you release endorphins, which is the feel-good hormone. It makes you happy for a little bit, which is exactly what you need.

Realize the Impact of Bullying

By this point, we all understand the negative impact that bullying can have on just about everyone.

According to Ditch the Label, of every 10 people who are bullied, three of them will self harm, one will go on to have a failed suicide attempt, and one will develop an eating disorder.

You don't want the weight of this on your shoulders. Remember that you're changing other people's lives. You have the power to turn that around.

You have all the right tools under your belt (including the fluorescent light tester, and yes, that's a thing).

The point is, you know everything you need to know to stop bullying. In case you need that extra push, read the following case study of what happened to two young boys that went from the ones being bullied to the ones doing the bullying (and in a deadly way).

Famous Case Studies

TWELVE

Columbine

Littleton, Colorado, April 20, 1999. Teenagers Eric Harris and Dylan Klebold entered Columbine High School armed with assault weapons and homemade bombs. The boys opened fire on everyone they saw.

They killed 12 classmates, a teacher, injured 18 other teenagers, and then shot and killed themselves. The people of Littleton had one major question: Why?

Investigations revealed that Harris and Klebold were constantly ridiculed and bullied at school. Another student falsely reported that they brought marijuana to school; their lockers were searched, bringing more ridicule upon them.

The boys were surrounded by schoolmates who doused them with ketchup and called them names while teachers watched (and didn't do anything about it). They wore the ketchup all day, unable to change clothes.

In his suicide note, Eric Harris indicated that he and Dylan Klebold had been continually bullied at school and were completely isolated from other students. "It's payback time," Eric wrote.

Virginia Tech

Blacksburg, Virginia, April 16, 2007. Twenty-three-year-old Seung-Hui Cho opened fire on the students and faculty at Virginia Tech University. After shooting at least 174 rounds, he killed 32 and wounded 25; then, he took his own life. He made history for being the cause of the deadliest shooting in the U.S.

Investigations revealed that Cho was a loner at school. He was declared mentally ill in 2005 and had to seek outpatient treatment. When he was in middle school and high school, he suffered bullying for his speech defects, causing him to develop selective mutism, an anxiety of speaking. Cho's suicide note showed his repressed anger toward "rich kids," "debauchery," and "deceitful charlatans."

In a video Cho sent to NBC news prior to the shootings, he declared, "You had a hundred billion chances and ways to have avoided today. But you decided to spill my blood. You forced me into a corner and gave me only one option. The decision was yours. Now you have blood on your hands that will never wash off."

Charles Manson

He was born "No-name Maddox" in 1934. His mother, Kathleen, was a teenage alcoholic and prostitute. Unwanted and unloved, his mother offered to sell him to a bartender for a pitcher of beer. His mother briefly married an older man who gave the child his last name: Manson.

Charles Milles Manson was left to fend for himself in life when he was six years old. Kathleen and her brother were in prison for robbing a gas station. Charlie was passed around from relative to relative who did not want him.

If Charlie cried about anything, his uncle called him a "sissy" and punished him by dressing him in girls' clothes and sending him to school.

"I was teased and hit so much; I went into a rage and started fighting everyone. [...] I was sick of being teased, laughed at, hit, kicked, and not allowed to play with the other boys. All that changed me."

Because his mother could not care for him, Charlie was made a ward of the court and placed in a religious-oriented school, the Gibault Home for Boys in Indiana. Discipline was strict at Gibault; for even minor infractions, Charlie, age 12, was whipped with a leather strap or wooden paddle.

Charlie described his life at Gibault: "I was a small kid. I was easy pickings for those who were inclined to be bullies. I saw a lot of things. I saw kids forced into homosexual acts. I was told all kinds of ways to beat the law. If you care too much about a part of your life, like me wanting to see my mom, others take advantage of it and ridicule you constantly."

Charles Manson's Ranch

Charlie ran away from Gibault, was caught, and was taken to the Indiana School for Boys in Plainfield, Indiana. Charlie was constantly in trouble for rule violations. The first night he was there, he was beaten and raped repeatedly by older boys. He alleged in his biography that the administrators of the school not only knew about the constant beatings and rapes, but they often encouraged such treatment for a troublemaker like Charlie.

He was a victim of bullying and severe sexual assaults; in turn, he himself raped and beat younger, smaller children. At Plainfield, rapes and beatings were like a spectator sport; the other boys and some staff members always observed these incidents. Charlie was released from Plainfield when he turned 18.

On the nights of August 9 and 10, 1969, a total of seven people were horrifically murdered and mutilated in a rich section of Los Angeles. Charles Manson ordered five members of his so-called "family" to commit these murders and told them exactly how to kill the victims. By the time of the Manson Murders, Charlie, at age 35, had been in jail most of his juvenile and adult life. He had no empathy for others. He was ruthless in his violent acts; these murders were the result of Charlie's desire to control others.

A national magazine called Charlie "the Most Dangerous Man Alive." Now 73 years old, he remains in jail in California. His last parole hearing was in 2007; none of the "Manson family" killers have ever been paroled; Charlie knows he will die in prison.

In the conclusion to his biography of Charles Manson, Nuel Emmons, who once served time with Charlie in prison, wrote, "What made Manson what he is? The unbroken chain of horrifying abuse and neglect from early childhood on doesn't explain it all, for others with an equally unhappy past have managed to escape his fate. Ultimately, the mystery of Manson's life and the man he became is a complex one that doesn't yield easily to examination. But somewhere in this story and his own words, some of the answers may begin to emerge, allowing us to see him, and perhaps some part of ourselves, more clearly" (1988).

Conclusion

Take two.

You're in the locker room, in your usual corner. You're getting ready to change, but you hesitate, as always, taking a moment to look around you to see if anyone is staring at you.

Your insecurity is heavy today, the weight of your bones fuller than normal. You turn back around and begin to lift your shirt.

You hear a snicker behind you, but you don't turn around. You want to keep your body facing the wall, because you've always hated the way your stomach looks.

You hear the click of a phone unlocking.

Heart pounding, knees locking, chest rising and falling faster than ever.

A flash reflects off the glistening red locker, and you hear muffled sounds, hands on mouths covering the melody of mocking laughs from the popular kids.

They've taken a picture of you.

"Hey," you hear someone say behind you, "what are you doing?"

You look down, afraid to turn around, but you know they're talking about you.

"What do you mean?" a voice says.

"You can't just take pictures of people like that," you hear.

At that, you turn around, stomach and all.

All eyes are on you.

You don't speak. You just look at the camera and back up into the eyes of the bully.

"Delete the picture," the bystander says.

"What picture?"

"The picture you just took of her. Delete it."

"I don't know what you're talking about," the bully says between snickers.

"Give me that," the bystander reaches for the phone, tapping and scrolling, and then hands it back.

"Put your shirt on, and let's go," the bystander says to you.

For the first time ever, you realize you won't be walking into gym class alone. And suddenly, everything feels a little different.

APPENDIX A

Bullying Statistics

Knowing the facts when it comes to bullying is really important in terms of stopping it. If you're interested in getting down to the numbers, here's a compiled list of statistics on bullying in the United States, courtesy the American Society for the Positive Care of Children (American SPCC).

National Statistics

28% of students in grades 6-12 have been bullied.

20% of students in grades 9-12 have been bullied.

About 30% of teens admit to bullying others.

70.6% of teens say they have seen bullying.

70.4% of school staff has seen bullying.

62% of school staff has seen bullying more than twice in the last month.

41% of school staff sees bullying once a week or more.

When bystanders do something, bullying stops within 10 seconds 57% of the time.

6% of students in grades 6-12 have been cyberbullied.

16% of high school students were cyberbullied in the last year.

55.2% of LGBT students have been cyberbullied.

60% of middle school students say they've been bullied, but only 16% of the staff believes that these students are bullied.

160,000 students don't go to school every day because of bullying.

30% of students who reported they'd been bullied said they had brought a weapon to school.

A bully is 6 times more likely to be in jail by the age of 24.

A bully is 5 times more likely to have a serious criminal record when he grows up.

2 out of 3 students who are targets become bullies themselves.

20% of all kids say they've been bullied.

20% of all high school students say they've seriously considered suicide within the past year.

25% of students say that teachers intervened in a bullying situation, but 71% of teachers say they intervene.

The average kid has watched 8,000 televised murders and 100,000 acts of violence before middle school starts.

If a school has an anti-bullying program, bullying is reduced by 50%.

Bullying was a factor in 2 out of 3 school shootings reviewed by the US Secret Service (there were 37 shootings total).

Since 1999, the Office on Violence against Women has spent $98 million in assistance to address campus sexual violence.

Bullying Statistics 2010 Report

There was a new round of bullying statistics done in 2010 that revealed that about 2.7 million students are bullied each year, and 2.1 million students take on the role of being a bully.

About 56% of all students have witnessed a bullying crime take place in school.

15% of all students who don't show up for school say it's because of bullying reasons.

71% of students report bullying is a serious, ongoing problem.

1 out of 10 students drops out or changes schools because of bullying.

1 out of every 20 students has seen a student with a gun at school.

The top years in school for bullying includes 4th through 8th grade. 90% report that they have been bullied.

54% of students report that witnessing physical abuse at home can lead to violence in school.

282,000 students are attacked in high schools each month.

Cyberbulling Statistics

According to the i-SAFE foundation, over half of teens have been bullied online.

More than 1 in 3 people have experienced threats online.

Over 25% of teens have been bullied through the use of cell phones.

Over half of victims do not tell their parents when online bullying is happening.

According to the Hartford County Examiner, 1 in 10 teens have had an embarrassing or damaging picture taken of themselves without their permission.

1 in 5 teens have posted or sent sexually explicit pictures of themselves.

Girls are more likely to be involved in cyberbullying than boys are.

According to the Cyberbulling Research Center, cyberbullying victims are more likely to have low self-esteem and to consider suicide.

Bullycide Statistics

Bullycide is death by suicide because of bullying. According to Make Beats Not Beat Downs (MBNBD), suicide is the leading cause of death for children under 14.

Since 2002, "at least 15 schoolchildren ages 11 to 14 have committed suicide in Massachusetts" (**http://makebeatsnotbeatdowns.org**).

Kids between 10 and 14 years of age have increasingly growing suicide rates — it's grown about 50% over the last 30 years.

Gay Bullying Statistics

Courtesy MBNBD, 86% of LGBT students say that they have been harassed at school in the last year.

9 out of 10 LGBT youth have been verbally harassed in the past year.

44.1% have been physically harassed.

22.1% have been physically assaulted.

60.8% did not report the harassment.

Of the students that did report the harassment, 31.1% said the staff did nothing about it.

A Checklist for Your School

If you see bullying happening at your school and want to take an extra step to stopping it, give this 25-question checklist to your teachers or school administrators.

This checklist is designed to start a discussion among school staff, parents, school board members, and legislatures. Each question can be answered "yes" or "no." "Maybe" answers indicate that the school needs to examine their anti-bullying policy to make certain it is in place and is working effectively.

1. Does the school work closely with parents by providing information about the school's anti-bullying established policy?

2. Is there a zero-tolerance policy against violence (verbal or physical) in the school?

3. Does the school publicize its anti-bullying policy in the local newspaper, newsletters to parents, and other means?

4. Does the school make clear to families and community members that a no-violence policy is expected in these environments, as well as in the school?

5. Is the school clear and consistent in dealing with bullying and bystanding incidents, especially those that could be considered criminal acts?

6. Does the school take notice of violence in other schools to avoid the "copycat" syndrome in their own school?

7. Has the school principal and school board members publicly spoken to media personnel about their efforts to make the school bully-free?

8. Does the school promote a friendly and kind atmosphere?

9. Has each student been informed about the school's anti-bullying policy?

10. Does the school promote personal responsibility for unkind actions towards other students?

11. Does the school have a policy against violent language and name-calling?

12. Does the school promote mediation between the bully and the victim to resolve the bullying incident or pattern in a conciliatory manner?

13. Are new students, staff, and school board members given information about the school's anti-bullying policy?

14. Are comprehensive records kept about each incident of bullying, such as the bully, the victim, and the bystanders, if known, for consistent monitoring?

15. Does the school provide staff hall monitors, cafeteria monitors, bathroom monitors, and monitors at school-sponsored activities?

16. Are groups like the Student Council actively involved in promoting anti-bullying policies?

17. Are both vulnerable and potentially violent students identified by the principal's or guidance counselor's office?

18. Is non-acceptance of bullying a prominent part of the curriculum for school classes?

19. Does the curriculum include lessons that foster self-esteem and respect for others?

20. Is media violence part of the school curriculum?

21. Is specific advice concerning personal safety a part of the curriculum?

22. Are problem-solving techniques that do not involve violence a part of the curriculum?

23. Are students taught what constitutes bullying and bystanding?

24. Are students taught how to be a good listener, how to be a reliable witness to incidents of bullying, how the law defines human rights, how to accept peers who are in some way different than other students, and the serious dangers of bullying?

25. Have the students, parents, and school staff all signed the pledge against toleration of bullying, and displayed those pledges in a prominent place?

The most important thing that your school can do is to make sure everyone is aware of bullying and its effects. A lot of people don't realize it's a problem, let alone what to do about it. Bring this forward to your principal and start making a change at your school.

A Student's Anti-Bullying Pledge

We, the students of _____ school, have decided to make our school free of bullying. We believe that all students have a right to an education and to receive that education in a safe environment. We define bullying as pushing, kicking, hitting, destroying personal property, stalking, cyberbullying, gang intimidation or violence, name-calling, making fun of others' differences, excluding someone from our peer group, and laughing at others. We pledge to:

1. Treat others with respect and accept their differences in race, religion, intelligence, gender, national origin, or color.

2. Never be involved in bullying incidents or be a bully.

3. Never be a bystander in bullying incidents.

4. Report all incidents of bullying to a school staff member.

5. Follow our school's anti-bullying policy.

6. Help our teachers and school administrators develop an anti-bullying policy.

7. Provide emotional support for someone who has been bullied.

8. Participate in all school activities that support our no-bullying policy.

9. Be a good role model for others by being kind, respectful, and non-violent.

My signature and date: _____

APPENDIX D

Bullying Laws

If you feel like you have a serious case of bullying going on at your school, consider getting the police involved. Here are some laws that might help you get some justice.

Right now, no federal laws exist that specifically address bullying. However, there are laws that address harassment. According to Stop Bullying, schools are obligated by these laws to address behavior that is:

- Severe, pervasive, or persistent
- Creates a hostile environment at school — that is, it is sufficiently serious that it interferes with or limits a student's ability to participate in or benefit from the services, activities, or opportunities offered by a school
- Based on a student's race, color, national origin, sex, disability, or religion
- Although the US Department of Education, under Title VI of the Civil Rights Act of 1964, does not directly cover religion, often religious based harassment is based on shared ancestry of ethnic characteristics, which *is* covered. The US

Department of Justice has jurisdiction over religion under Title IV of the Civil Rights Act of 1964.

If a school doesn't act when a situation like this happens, they may be violating civil rights, which include the following:

- Title IV and Title VI of the Civil Rights Act of 1964
- Title IX of the Education Amendments of 1972
- Section 504 of the Rehabilitation Act of 1973
- Titles II and III of the Americans with Disabilities Act
- Individuals with Disabilities Education Act (IDEA)

There are also civil rights that help to protect the LBGT community, which include:

- Title IX and Title IV do not prohibit discrimination based solely on sexual orientation, but they protect all students, including students who are LGBT or perceived to be LGBT, from sex-based harassment.
- Harassment based on sex and sexual orientation are not mutually exclusive. When students are harassed based on their actual or perceived sexual orientation, they may also be subjected to forms of sex discrimination recognized under Title IX.

A school is obligated to follow certain steps when they receive a formal complaint, which includes the following:

- Immediate and appropriate action to investigate or otherwise determine what happened
- Inquiry must be prompt, thorough, and impartial

- Interview targeted students, offending students, and witnesses, and maintain written documentation of investigation
- Communicate with targeted students regarding steps taken to end harassment
- Check in with targeted students to ensure that harassment has stopped

The school district must be on notice in order to be sued. To put a school district on notice, you just have to bring the bullying to their attention in some way. In bullying cases, usually the school district or even an individual teacher is sued for not taking action.

If the harassment doesn't stop, you can take legal action by filing a formal grievance with the district and contacting the U.S. Department of Education's Office for Civil Rights and from the U.S. Department of Justice's Civil Rights Division. These can be found at **www2.ed.gov/about/offices/list/ocr/index.html** and at **www.justice.gov/crt/how-file-complaint#three**.

References

"Barack Obama Shares Childhood Tales at Bullying Conference." *The Telegraph*. Telegraph Media Group, 10 Mar. 2011. Web. 09 Mar. 2016.

"Bully Facts & Statistics." *Bully Facts & Statistics*. Make Beats Not Beat Downs. Web. 09 Mar. 2016.

"Bullying Statistics 2010." *Bullying Statistics*. Bullying Statistics, 07 July 2015. Web. 09 Mar. 2016.

"Bullying Statistics and Information." *American SPCC*. American SPCC. Web. 09 Mar. 2016.

"Cyber Bullying Statistics." *Bullying Statistics*. Bullying Statistics, 07 July 2015. Web. 09 Mar. 2016.

"Dissociative Amnesia." *Center for Behavioral Health*. Cleveland Clinic, Apr. 2012. Web. 08 Mar. 2016.

"Eyes on Bullying." *Eyes on Bullying*. Education Development Center, Inc., 2008. Web. 08 Mar. 2016.

"Federal Laws." *Federal Laws.* Stop Bullying, 31 Mar. 2014. Web. 09 Mar. 2016.

"Mean Stinks." *Mean Stinks.* Secret. Web. 08 Mar. 2016.

"Military Career." *The Official Website of the British Monarchy.* The Royal Household. Web. 09 Mar. 2016.

"Police: As Many as 20 Present at Gang Rape outside School Dance." *CNN.* Cable News Network, 28 Oct. 2009. Web. 09 Mar. 2016.

"Two High School Football Players Tackle Bullying." *The Meredith Vieira Show.* Web. 08 Mar. 2016.

Anonymous. "My Bullying Experience." *Reach Out.* Reachout.com, Mar. 2011. Web. 9 Mar. 2016.

Bazelon, Emily. *Sticks and Stones: Defeating the Culture of Bullying and Rediscovering the Power of Character and Empathy.* New York: Random House, 2013. Print.

Bear, George G., et al. "Differences In Bullying Victimization Between Students With And Without Disabilities." *School Psychology Review* 44.1 (2015): 98. *MasterFILE Premier.* Web. 7 Mar. 2016.

Bradshaw, Catherine P., et al. "Bullies, Gangs, Drugs, And School: Understanding The Overlap And The Role Of Ethnicity And Urbanicity." *Journal Of Youth And Adolescence* 42.2 (2013): 220-234. *ERIC.* Web. 7 Mar. 2016.

Burkley, Melissa. "Why Don't We Help? Less Is More, at Least When It Comes to Bystanders." *Psychology Today*. Psychology Today, 4 Nov. 2009. Web. 09 Mar. 2016.

Chase, Chris. "22 Facts about Michael Phelps' Record 22 Olympic Medals." *Yahoo! Sports*. Yahoo!, 4 Aug. 2012. Web. 9 Mar. 2016.

Coloroso, Barbara. The Bully, the Bullied, and the Bystander: From Preschool to High School: How Parents and Teachers Can Help Break the Cycle of Violence. New York: HarperResource, 2003. Print.

Cyrus, Miley, and Hilary Liftin. *Miles to Go*. New York: Disney/ Hyperion, 2009. Print.

Gansberg, Martin. "37 Who Saw Murder Didn't Call the Police." *The New York Times*. The New York Times, 26 Mar. 1964. Web. 09 Mar. 2016.

Gardener, Stephanie S. C. "Stress and Sweat: Stay Cool Under Fire." *WebMD*. WebMD, 27 Nov. 2015. Web. 08 Mar. 2016.

Garrett, Anne G. *Bullying in American Schools: Causes, Preventions, Interventions*. Jefferson, NC: McFarland, 2003. Print.

Halligan, John, and Kelly Halligan. "Ryan's Story Presentation." Ryan's Story Presentation LTD. Web. 08 Mar. 2016.

Hirschberg, Lynn. "From the Vaults: The Fall & Rise of Christina Aguilera." *W Magazine*. July 2011. Web. 08 Mar. 2016.

Hoover, John H., and Ronald Oliver. *The Bullying Prevention Handbook: A Guide for Principals, Teachers, and Counselors*. Bloomington, IN: National Education Service, 1996. Print.

Horrevorts, Esther, et al. "The Relation Between Bullying And Subclinical Psychotic Experiences And The Influence Of The Bully Climate Of School Classes." *European Child & Adolescent Psychiatry* 23.9 (2014): 765-772 8p. *CINAHL with Full Text*. Web. 7 Mar. 2016.

Irvine, Chris. "Clever Boys 'Dumb Down' to Avoid Being Bullied, Study Claims." *The Telegraph*. Telegraph Media Group, 29 Mar. 2009. Web. 09 Mar. 2016.

Lane, Derrick. "Chris Rock: 'Bullying Made Me Who I Am.'" *Black America Web RSS*. Interactive One, 10 Feb. 2014. Web. 09 Mar. 2016.

Levine, Stuart. "Can 'The Voice' Be Heard?" *Variety*. Variety Media, 09 Apr. 2011. Web. 08 Mar. 2016.

Manson, Charles, and Nuel Emmons. *Manson in His Own Words*. New York, NY: Grove, 1986. Print.

McCollum, Carmen. "Bullying: One Girl's Story." *Nwitimes.com*. NWI Times, 9 Jan. 2012. Web. 09 Mar. 2016.

McGrath, Mary Jo. *School Bullying: Tools for Avoiding Harm and Liability*. Thousand Oaks, CA: Corwin, 2007. Print.

Messer, Lesley. "Taylor Swift Suffered Bullying in School." *PEOPLE. com*. Time Inc., 27 Jan. 2009. Web. 09 Mar. 2016.

Michael. "Living with Asperger's Syndrome." *Reach Out*. Reachout. com, Sept. 2011. Web. 9 Mar. 2016.

Miller, Holly Ventura, and J. Mitchell Miller. "School-Based Bullying Prevention." *Encyclopedia of Victimology and Crime Prevention. Fight Crime*. FightCrime.org. Web.

NewsOne Staff. "How Many Medals Does Michael Phelps Have?" *News One How Many Medals Does Michael PhelpsHave Comments*. Interactive One, 13 Aug. 2012. Web. 09 Mar. 2016.

Olweus, Dan. *Bullying at School: What We Know and What We Can Do*. Maiden, MA: Blackwell Pub., 1993. Print.

Perlstein, Linda. *Not Much, Just Chillin: The Hidden Lives of Middle Schoolers*. New York: Farrar, Straus and Giroux, 2003. Print.

Randel, Derek. *Stopping School Violence: The Complete Guide for Parents and Educators on Handling Bullying*. Bloomington, IN: Authorhouse, 2006. Print.

Reporter, Daily Mail. "'I Was Bullied at School over My Funny-looking Face,' Reveals Black Swan Beauty Mila Kunis." *Mail Online*. Associated Newspapers, 11 Feb. 2011. Web. 09 Mar. 2016.

Sigurdson, Johannes Foss, et al. "The Long-Term Effects Of Being Bullied Or A Bully In Adolescence On Externalizing And Internalizing Mental Health Problems In Adulthood." *Child &*

Adolescent Psychiatry & Mental Health 9.1 (2015): 1-13. *Academic Search Complete.* Web. 7 Mar. 2016.

Simmons, Rachel. *Odd Girl Out: The Hidden Culture of Aggression in Girls.* New York: Harcourt, 2002. Print.

STOMP Out Bullying. "Anti-Gay Bullying." STOMP Out Bullying. Web. 08 Mar. 2016.

STOMP Out Bullying. "Why Do Kids Bully?" STOMP Out Bullying. Web. 08 Mar. 2016.

Trust, Gary. "Ask Billboard: Taylor Swift Out-'Shake's Mariah Carey." *Billboard.* Billboard, 1 Sept. 2014. Web. 08 Mar. 2016.

U.S. Department of Health & Human Services. "Effects of Bullying." *Effects of Bullying.* Stop Bullying. Web. 08 Mar. 2016.

U.S. Department of Health & Human Services. "What You Can Do." *What You Can Do.* Stop Bullying. Web. 08 Mar. 2016.

Weiser, Benjamin. "Pine Bush School District Settles Anti-Semitism Suit for $4.48 Million." *The New York Times.* The New York Times, 29 June 2015. Web. 09 Mar. 2016.

Glossary

A

Accountability Holding someone responsible for his or her actions.

Aggression Acting out, often in a violent manner, toward people and/or animals.

Anti-bullying A stance that is against bullying in all its forms.

Anti-Bullying Act of 2005 (H.R. 284) A bill that was introduced in the House of Representatives that includes cyberbullying in its definition of bullying behavior if the bullying is done on school computers and other forms of technology.

Anti-Semitism Prejudice against, hatred of, or discrimination against Jews as an ethnic, religious, or racial group.

Anti-Social Personality Disorder A psychiatric condition in which the sufferer violates the rights of others or does not conform to socially acceptable behavior.

Asperger's Syndrome A developmental disorder affecting the ability to effectively socialize and communicate.

Assault A physical attack on another person.

B

Backbiting Malicious talk about someone who is not present.

Blame The act of holding another person or group responsible for your actions or faults.

Bully The tormenting of others by using verbal harassment, physical assault, or even other methods such as manipulation and gossip.

Bully-proof A term used to describe children who are immune to bullying, whether naturally or by instruction.

Bullycide A suicide as the result of bullying.

Bystander A person who observes but does not participate; bystanders may serve as enablers of bullies.

Bystander effect A social psychological phenomenon that refers to cases in which individuals do not offer any means of help to a victim when other people are present.

C

Civil rights Those rights established to all United States citizens through the thirteenth and fourteenth amendments. It is often used in reference to the rights that were extended to minority groups.

Common Concern Method A method of working with bullies and victims that is designed to lessen the pathological impact of bullying on children and that helps bullies understand the feelings of their victims and helps all parties involved reach a solution.

Conduct Disorder A mental health disorder that is often diagnosed in infancy, childhood, or adolescence that is characterized by a pattern of behavior in which the basic rights of others or societal norms are violated.

Cyberbullying A form of bullying that is perpetrated on the Internet, especially via e-mail, instant messenger, and chat rooms.

D

Depression A state of mental health characterized by extreme melancholy, sadness, and inadequacy.

Dissociative Amnesia A mental illness that involves disruptions or breakdowns of memory, consciousness, awareness, identity, and/or perception.

Domestic violence A form of physical, emotional, and verbal abuse directed towards one's significant other.

G

Genocide The deliberate killing of a large group of people, especially those of a particular ethnic group or nation.

H

Harassment To make repeated attacks against someone in an effort to disturb or hurt him or her.

Hate crime A crime perpetrated against someone based on his or her race, gender, religion, sexual orientation, etc.

Hippo An analogy used to help break down the denial of a problem and to help acknowledge that it needs to be addressed.

Holocaust The systematic, bureaucratic, state-sponsored persecution and murder of six million Jews by the Nazi regime and its collaborators; means "sacrifice by fire."

Hypervigilence A state of heightened sensory sensitivity that allows one to detect threats.

I

Insanity defense A defense by excuse in criminal trials arguing that the defendant is not responsible for their actions due to an episodic or persistent psychiatric illness.

Intervention An attempt, whether by one person or a group, to stop a certain action; in this case, bullying.

Intimidation A technique that combines threats and fear used to make a weaker person do something.

Isolation Separation from a person or a group, especially socially.

J

Juvenile Justice System The legal system in which juveniles are processed, adjudicated, and corrected.

M

Mean girls A type of bullying perpetrated by girls in which backstabbing, exclusion, and rumors are used to isolate and terrorize a victim.

Mental health The condition of psychological stability.

Mobbing The act of several bullies working together to harm their target.

N

Negligence As related to bullying, the act of a school employee failing to act to prevent bullying and to protect victims, especially because they have a duty to do so.

P

Peer group A grouping of people based on their age.

Pluralistic ignorance A situation in which a majority of group members privately reject a norm, but incorrectly assume that most others accept it, and therefore go along with it.

Post-Traumatic Stress Syndrome A condition characterized in which a person often relives traumatic events from his or her past.

R

Racial slur A disparaging remark made about someone's skin color.

Red flag A term used to describe warning signs that a child is a bully or is the victim of bullying.

Rumor Misinformation that is maliciously spread in order to isolate someone.

S

Self-esteem A person's sense of self-worth; how much he or she values his or herself.

Sexual harassment A form of harassment in which the victim is subjected to unwanted sexual comments and advances.

Stalking The act of purposely and repeatedly following and harassing another person.

Substance abuse The use of any addictive substance (such as drugs or alcohol) for non-therapeutic purposes.

Suicide The act of taking one's own life.

Supreme Court The highest court in the United States as established by Article III of the constitution. The rulings of the nine justices determine precedents for cases heard by lower courts.

T

Target A person who is the aim of a bully, especially for ridiculing and exploitative purposes.

Tattletale A person who reports others' wrongdoings to an authority figure.

Truancy The failure of a child to attend school, especially an absence that is not legitimate.

U

Unconditional love The act of loving someone regardless of his or her actions or beliefs.

V

Victim The person against whom a crime was committed; in this case, the target of a bully.

W

Witness A person who sees an event take place.

Z

Zero tolerance A policy that strictly enforces the rules and/or laws.

Index